The Photoshop ELEMENTS 5 Restoration & Retouching Book

by Matt Kloskowski

**The Photoshop® Elements 5
Restoration & Retouching Book Team**

CREATIVE DIRECTOR
Felix Nelson

TECHNICAL EDITORS
Kim Doty
Cindy Snyder

TRAFFIC DIRECTOR
Kim Gabriel

PRODUCTION MANAGER
Dave Damstra

**COVER DESIGN AND
CREATIVE CONCEPTS**
Jessica Maldonado

**COVER PHOTOS
COURTESY OF**
Carl Zumbano, Fotolia,
and iStockphoto

PUBLISHED BY
Peachpit Press

Composed in Avenir (Linotype), Bradley Hand (International Typeface Corporation), CAC Pinafore (American Greetings Corporation), and Dalliance Roman (Emigre) by NAPP Publishing.

Trademarks
All terms mentioned in this book that are known to be trademarks or service marks have been appropriately capitalized. Peachpit Press cannot attest to the accuracy of this information. Use of a term in the book should not be regarded as affecting the validity of any trademark or service mark.

Macintosh is a registered trademark of Apple Computer.
Windows is a registered trademark of Microsoft Corporation.
Photoshop Elements is a registered trademark of Adobe Systems Incorporated.

Warning and Disclaimer
This book is designed to provide information about Photoshop Elements. Every effort has been made to make this book as complete and as accurate as possible, but no warranty of fitness is implied.

The information is provided on an as-is basis. The author and Peachpit Press shall have neither liability nor responsibility to any person or entity with respect to any loss or damages arising from the information contained in this book or from the use of the discs or programs that may accompany it.

ISBN 0-321-48165-8
9 8 7 6 5 4 3 2 1

Printed and bound in the United States of America

www.peachpit.com
www.scottkelbybooks.com

For my wife Diana.
It's been eight years since
we first met, and I still
thank my lucky stars that
we were brought together.

Acknowledgments

First, I'd like to thank one of the most important people in my life—my incredibly beautiful, funny, caring, sensitive, and fun-loving wife, Diana. I have the easy job. I get to go to work every day to do what I love and get paid for it. She works 10 times as hard as I do and never seems to wear down. I'll always be grateful for the wonderful job you do raising our kids each day while still managing to have an ear-to-ear smile on your face when I come home. You're the best wife a guy could hope for.

Next, I owe more thanks than they'll ever know to my two sons, Ryan and Justin. The two of you put things into perspective for me in ways that you'll never be aware of and just make me the absolute proudest dad I could have ever hoped to be. No matter how much I work, what I write, or whatever I do, my favorite thing in the world is still hanging out with my two buddies. I wouldn't trade it for anything.

None of this would be worth anything without people to share it with and I'm lucky enough to have the best family a guy could hope for. First, thanks go to my mom and dad for giving me such a great start and encouraging me to do whatever it was I wanted in life. I'd also like to thank my brother and sister and their spouses: Ed, Kerry, Kristine, and Scott. You've all been such a positive influence in my life and your support means the world to me.

I'd also like to thank Scott Kelby. One day I got a call asking me to come talk to Scott about a permanent position with the National Association of Photoshop Professionals. That day changed my career and my life, and I owe a great debt to Scott. All I can say is thank you. You've not only given me tremendous opportunities, but you've become a great friend and role model of mine in the process, and I'm honestly not sure which to be more thankful for.

To Dave Moser, your constant nudging… wait, let's call it what it really is—flat out pushing—is what makes this book and everything else I do better and better. Thanks for always reminding me to strive to be better, but more importantly, thanks for becoming a great buddy as well.

I'd also like to thank Dave Cross. Dave has become a great friend of mine over the last few years. He's a constant reminder to me of a true professional in this industry. If there is any person to follow personally, professionally, and ethically, Dave is the one.

I don't know what I would have done without our two tech and copy editors, Cindy Snyder and Kim Doty. The two of you are editing machines and you do it all with a smile on your face (and I know I'm not that funny). I can only imagine how hard it is to put each tutorial through the testing it needs. I truly appreciate all of your hard work to make this book the best, but also in making me look better as well.

Special thanks go to Felix Nelson, Dave Damstra, and Jessica Maldonado. The book you're holding in your hands looks as great as it does because of them and their amazing ideas. They take a bunch of text and turn it into the amazing book you're holding right now. There's no doubt these guys are the best in the industry. Thanks also go to Kim Gabriel for keeping this project, and the many others she juggles, on track.

Many thanks go to Ted Waitt, Scott Cowlin, and Nancy Ruenzel at Peachpit Press for continuing to be leaders in this industry and giving me the opportunity to do what I love to do.

Finally, I owe special thanks to you, the reader. I had a blast writing this book. While I knew I would enjoy writing on this topic when I started the book, I had no idea just how much. Without your support though, through emails, phone calls, and of course the bookstores, I wouldn't be living my dream every day. Thank you.

thicken hair

Table of Contents

Table of Contents

Remove Braces

Table of Contents

Nana's old photos—
need lightening
and cleaning up.

Table of Contents

repair and clean up

Read This Before You Read the Rest of the Book

Well folks, lots of books have long introductions that tell you all about the book. I've decided to forgo that introduction (because I don't really think many people read them), and just list a few quick frequently asked questions (FAQs, for you acronym lovers). They're quick, short, and to the point, so make sure you read them.

Q. Can I download the images you've used in the book to follow along?

A. Of course. Just go to www.photoshoptraining.com/mattkloskowski to download them.

Q. What version of Photoshop Elements do I need for this book?

A. Ah…I knew you were going to ask that. I wrote this book with one major goal in mind: make as much of it as possible work for Photoshop Elements versions 3, 4, and 5. I was very successful and can tell you that 95% of what you'll read here works in all three of those versions. There are a few tutorials that only work in version 5, but I've added an "Elements 5 Only" symbol to tell you which ones they are. You'll also notice the screen captures were taken in version 5. Don't let this scare you away. Even though the color of the interface is different, the way things are laid out is practically identical.

Q. Is this book for beginners or advanced users?

A. I think it's for anyone that can follow step-by-step tutorials. The book is written in a recipe format. I kept thinking to myself, "How would I explain this tutorial to a family member?" and wrote it that way. I figured I wouldn't sit down with my mom and tell her to open the Levels adjustment and then follow it up by giving her a 10-minute dissertation on what Levels really is. Instead, I would tell her to open the Levels adjustment dialog and drag the white slider to the left. So that's how the book is written. I don't bog you down with details and lengthy explanations—just the fun stuff.

Q. How should I read this book?

A. Any way you want. You already bought it, so I'm not going to impose any rules on you. It's your money, so read it backwards for all I care. Okay, I'm just kidding here. You really can read the book any way you want though. It's written in a way that you can jump in anywhere. I will say, there are a few tutorials in the book where I use an image from a previous tutorial because I want to show a way to take that image even further with other techniques in the book. However, in all cases I mention what tutorial the image came from so you can go back and do that tutorial as well if you'd like. Other than that, jump right into a place that interests you and have a blast.

Adjust Color

Chapter 1

Fixing Exposure and Color Issues

One of the very first steps in retouching photos is getting the exposure and color to look right. Without a good base to work from, all of your retouching work becomes harder and less effective. In this chapter, we'll cover two of the most common problems you'll encounter when you have photos of people: (1) the people are too dark, and (2) the people are too light. We'll also take a look at how to fix the color in your photos. By getting these two basic aspects of your photos (exposure and color) corrected right from the beginning, you'll be amazed at just how good your photos will look.

Making Dark Photos Lighter

I'm kicking off the book with a tutorial that addresses one of the most common problems with digital photos today. Seriously, it happens to everyone. You take the photo only to get it onto your computer and find that the person (or photo) is too dark (i.e., underexposed). Fortunately, the folks that make Adobe Photoshop Elements know this is a common problem and have incorporated a number of easy ways to fix it.

METHOD 1: The Easy Way

STEP 1:
Open a photo that has too many shadowy areas or where the subject is just plain too dark.

STEP 2:
Go to the Enhance menu and choose Adjust Lighting>Shadows/Highlights. You should see an immediate change to your photo because the Lighten Shadows setting is already set to 25%. Notice the other two settings are set to 0%, so they won't do anything un- less you want them to. If you find that Elements did too much lightening of the dark areas, then just drag the Light- en Shadows slider to the left to reduce it. However, if you find that you need to lighten the dark areas even more, then just drag the slider to the right and it'll increase the effect. Beware, though, if you go too high with this setting you'll probably start to make your photo look worse in other ways. Remember, it's all about balance.

Lighten Shadows 2.jpg @ 66.7% (RGB/8*)

66.67%

MATT KLOSKOWSKI

METHOD 2: The Less Easy but More Controlled Way

STEP 1:
Okay, this method takes a little more getting used to but you get great results. Open another photo that suffers from too many dark areas.

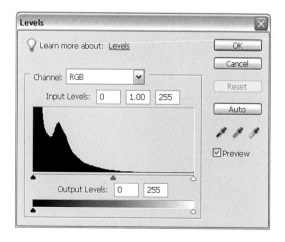

STEP 2:
Go under the Enhance menu again and choose Adjust Lighting>Levels (or press Ctrl-L [Mac: Command-L]). By the way, this may be a good time to point out that most of the things you do to adjust lighting and color problems with your photos will fall under this menu, so get acquainted with it. Now, at this point you should see the Levels dialog. If you're familiar with what a histogram is then this dialog may look familiar. If not, don't worry at all because it's still really simple to use.

Continued

STEP 3:

All you really need to do is drag the white slider on the right in toward the center. The best results will come if you start dragging it to the point where the small mountainous area starts to appear. Don't go too far into it though, or you'll start making the photo too light.

STEP 4:

Just like in the first method, you can always pull back and make the photo darker again by moving that same slider toward the right. Again, I find that the best results come when you get that slider right to the tip of the small mountain area (aka: histogram) that starts forming.

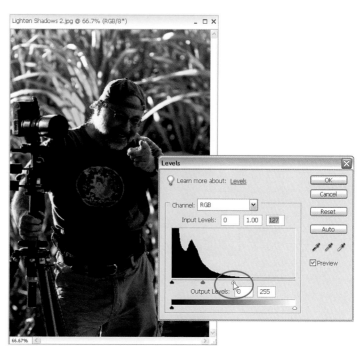

I'll often see people unhappy with their photos. They know something doesn't look right, but they just can't pinpoint it. When a photo is too dark, it's pretty obvious because you just can't see the people. However, when a photo is too light, it's not always apparent that too much light is the culprit. This often happens when you take a photo of a person outdoors right smack in the middle of the day. Most people don't realize that those extremely bright, sunlit areas take away from the photo and make it almost difficult to look at.

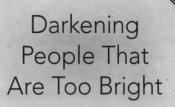

Darkening People That Are Too Bright

STEP 1:
Open a photo where the person is just too bright. I'm going to go out on a limb here and guess that this photo was taken outside in extreme sunlight. Or, it could be a photo that was taken in an already well-lit area with the on-camera flash turned on. Either way, if you see skin that almost looks white, then you've got a photo to work with.

STEP 2:
Just like the previous technique, we're going to go to the Shadows/Highlights adjustment under Enhance>Adjust Lighting>Shadows/Highlights. This time, move the Lighten Shadows slider all the way to the left to 0%. Then start moving the Darken Highlights slider toward the right and you'll see the really bright areas start to become darker. So how do you know where to stop? Generally, somewhere between 25–30% works well. If you go any higher, the person in your photo may begin to look as if they have a bad sunburn.

Continued

STEP 3:

Finally, sometimes adjusting the Darken Highlights slider can cause the entire photo to look, well, blah is the only word I can think of. Actually, "blah" is the technical term for lack of contrast. You can fix this by increasing the contrast, so move the Midtone Contrast slider toward the right to about 20%, or until your photo looks like it has a little more pop to it.

TIP: This is more of a guideline while taking photos than it is an Elements tip. You can avoid situations like the one in this tutorial altogether by trying your best not to photograph people in direct sunlight. If you do, then you're going to get some really harsh lighting. If at all possible, try moving to a slightly shaded area under an overhang or tree and you'll probably get a much better shot.

Before

After

For better or worse, our digital cameras often make decisions for us. Most of the time it's for the better, since the last thing we want to worry about when taking a photo is all of the technical details surrounding exposure and white balance. However, the camera doesn't always make the best decisions and we're left with photos that are slightly off-color. But how do you know if they're off-color? Often you can tell just by looking at the photo, but there are ways you can find out what's wrong with your photo in Elements as well.

How to Spot Photos That Are Off-Color

STEP 1:

Open a photo that you suspect is off-color or has a color cast to it. When you're working with photos of people you can generally look at the skin and judge whether it has that nice warm yellow/red color or if it has tints of green, blue, or even too much yellow, which often happens when taking photos indoors with no flash. In this example, the camera had the wrong white balance setting, which produced a very greenish-color photo.

STEP 2:

One way to spot whether or not you really have a problem is to examine areas in the photo that you know to be a specific color. Here, the bride's dress should be white. So grab your Eyedropper tool (I) and click on the dress to set your Foreground color to that sampled color. If you look in the bottom of the Toolbox at the Foreground color swatch, you'll see that color is more green than it is white. This is your first indicator that there's a problem.

Continued

STEP 3:

Try it with another photo. Here's a picture of my buddy Corey Barker. The overall photo (including the skin) is just too red. There's really no white point in the photo, but his shirt was black when I took the shot. So grab the Eyedropper tool and click on his shirt to see what color it is.

Corey_Color_Problem.jpg @ 50% (RGB/8)

50%

MATT KLOSKOWSKI

STEP 4:

As you can see, the color isn't really black but more of a reddish brown. Again, this should alert you to a potential color cast problem. Now that you know how to identify a color cast, read on to the next tutorial to see how to fix it.

At this point, you should know how to identify a color problem in your photo. Why? Because you just read the previous tutorial. If you didn't, then that means you're skipping around and that's not allowed here. Okay...kidding. Feel free to skip around all you'd like. Here we're going to take a look at how we can fix the skin color in our photos and remove any color casts that may exist.

Fixing a Color Cast

METHOD 1: The Easy Way

STEP 1:
Like many things, of course, there's an easy way and a less easy way. Oh yeah, if you haven't noticed, I try to avoid saying "difficult." It's the marketer inside me, I think. Actually, though, the more difficult way (oops, I said it) really isn't that hard—it's just a few more clicks than the easy way, but I'll do the easy way first. Let's open the same photo with the bride that we looked at in the previous tutorial.

STEP 2:
Go to Enhance>Adjust Lighting>Levels, or just press Ctrl-L (Mac: Command-L). This opens the Levels dialog. Levels is actually a really powerful adjustment, as there's a lot we can do with it. Here, we're going to use it to fix the color. Notice the three small Eyedropper icons right under the Auto button.

Continued

STEP 3:

Remember in the previous tutorial when we found an area that was supposed to be white and clicked on it only to find it was green? Well, the highlight Eyedropper works kind of the same way. You click on an area in the photo that should be white to set a white point. So, click on the third Eyedropper (the one half-filled with white) and then click on a bright area of the wedding dress. Elements knows that you're telling it that you want this color (which, if you remember, had a green tint to it) to be white and it makes the change for you. Cool stuff, huh?

Before

After

METHOD 2: The Slightly More Difficult Way (but Still Not Hard)

STEP 1:

Open another photo that doesn't have such a clear white area like the previous one. The photo of Corey that we looked at previously doesn't really have a white area at all. It does have a black area (his shirt) but it's also got a black background (which is really black), so this makes things a little more difficult to work with.

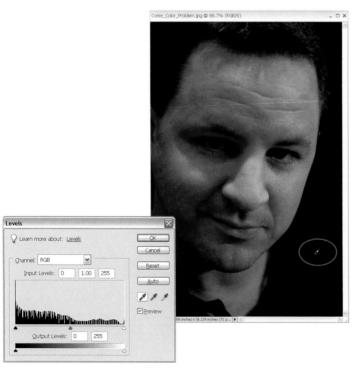

STEP 2:

In the previous tutorial, we sampled the color of the shirt only to find that it had a brownish/reddish tint to it. Working on what we've learned so far, you may think that you can open the Levels dialog just like before. Then you'd think you could click on the shadows Eyedropper (the half-black one) and click on the black shirt to set the black point and fix everything. If you look at this image, you'll see that isn't the case though.

Continued

STEP 3:

Now we'll have to resort to another method. First, duplicate the Background layer by pressing Ctrl-J (Mac: Command-J). You'll see two copies of the image in the Layers palette (Background and Layer 1).

STEP 4:

Then, click once on the top copy to select it. Go to the Filter menu and choose Blur>Average. Elements blurs the entire photo so much that you're just left with one single color—it's the average color of the photo which, as you can see here, has a strong reddish brown color to it. That makes sense since we identified this photo as having a red color cast.

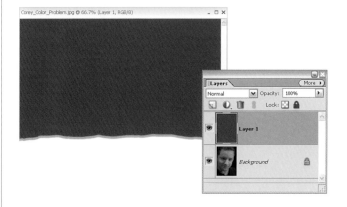

SUPER GEEK TIP: Feel free to skip this if you don't care about the theory behind what's happening. The way we fix the photo is by neutralizing this red color. Remember back to your color theory days? Me neither, but don't worry, this one is simple. To neutralize a color, you pick the opposite color on a color wheel. Take a look at this example of a color wheel. Our red is on one side and note that green/blue is the color directly opposite it on the color wheel. That means that a green/blue color will help us fix this photo.

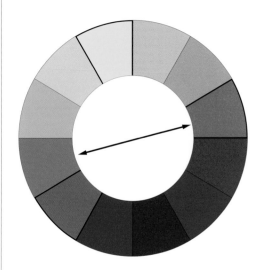

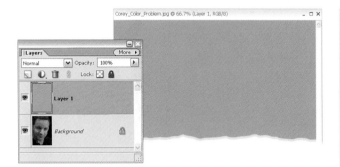

STEP 5:

Choose Filter>Adjustments>Invert and that will change the red color to a color that is directly opposite it in the whole color spectrum—in this case a greenish blue.

STEP 6:

Lastly, just change the blend mode of this color layer to Overlay and drop the opacity down to around 40–50%. The greenish blue from that layer will start to force the red out of the photo and your color cast is gone.

TIP: If you've got an outdoor photo with a color cast to it, I've found that changing the blend mode to Color will work as well.

Before

After

Removing That Yellowish Color from a Photo

Here's a problem I see everywhere: You're indoors and it's slightly dark. You pull out the camera and take a picture using the on-camera flash. You look at the photo and decide the flash is just way too much light, so you turn it off. From that point on, every photo you shoot has this yellowish color to it. "For God's sake, why?" you cry. Well, it's basically because the lights in your house give off a yellow color and it gets reflected in the photos. Luckily there's an easy fix for it.

STEP 1:

Open a photo that has that yellowish color to it. This is a picture of my lovely wife Diana. Mind you, she's perfect. Color problems from the camera (remember, it's the camera's fault) would be the only possible fix that anyone could do to her. And ya know what? She even looks awesome when she's yellow. But alas, I needed a photo to get my wife into a retouching book that wouldn't get me in a lotta trouble.

TIP: By the way, don't mind the flower in front of her. It was a Hawaiian-themed party and she had a drink in her hand that she felt compelled to hold up. Notice the happy smile on her face?

STEP 2:

Go under the Enhance menu and choose Adjust Color>Adjust Color for Skin Tone.

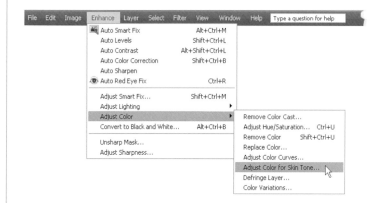

STEP 3:

This opens a dialog that is probably one of the easiest to use in Elements. All you need to do is click on an area of skin that is off-color. I find the best results when clicking on the forehead. That's probably because the cheek color can often be misleading. Also, the color of woman's makeup in certain areas of the face can throw the adjustment off. So, the forehead seems to be the best bet.

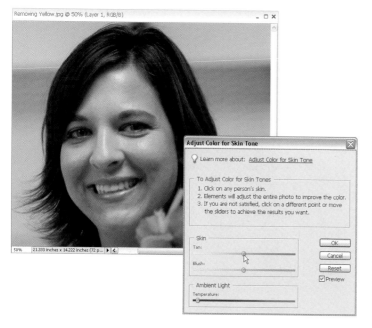

STEP 4:

And just like that, the skin color is much better. Just turn the Preview checkbox on and off to see the difference. Also, feel free to experiment with the Tan and Blush sliders. They do exactly what they say. The Tan slider adds more of a tan color and the Blush slider adds more of a pinkish color.

Continued

Before

After

remove spot glare from glasses & enhance eye color.

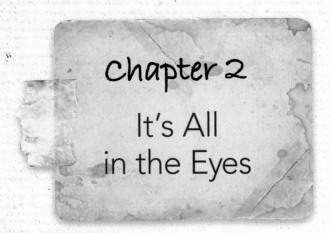

chapter 2

It's All
in the Eyes

If you're like most people, one of the first things you look at in a photo are the eyes. This is probably because we subconsciously know that the eyes can speak volumes about a person's mood and overall feeling. That's why it's so important that we make those eyes perfect. They need to stand out and make an impact. In this chapter, we'll take a look at several ways to make all aspects of the eyes do just that.

Whitening the Eyes

Ever take a photo of someone and find that the white parts of their eyes just don't look that white? Well, if you haven't, then come on over to one of my family gatherings and snap some shots because ours always seem to turn out that way. It's something that we really don't notice when we're looking at someone in person. However, when the photo is the only thing we have to look at, it becomes more apparent. Fortunately, there's a really easy way to make the whites of the eyes whiter.

STEP 1:

Open a photo where the white parts of the eyes just aren't all that white. Most of the time they'll either be: (a) bloodshot; (b) a grayish color; or (c) a demon-colored red, but I usually only see that in my kids' eyes so I wouldn't worry about it if I were you.

Whitening Eyes.jpg @ 100% (RGB/8)

100%   6.833 inches x 5.125 inches (72 ppi)

©FOTOLIA

STEP 2:

Create a duplicate of the Background layer by pressing Ctrl-J (Mac: Command-J). Now you'll see two layers in the Layers palette, the Background layer and Layer 1.

STEP 3:

Select the Dodge tool (press O until you have it). If you've never used this one before, it's grouped in the very last tool set in the Toolbox. It almost looks like an all-black magnifying glass. Then, in the Options Bar, set the Range to Midtones and the Exposure to 50%.

STEP 4:

Click once on the top layer to select it and zoom in on the eyes (with the Zoom tool [Z]) if necessary. Start painting with the Dodge tool over the white parts of the eyes. It'll probably just take a few strokes so don't go too crazy. If you go too white, then the person will look like an alien. We're just looking for subtle changes here. Switch over to the other eye and do the same thing. Oh, and try not to paint too much over the colored parts of the eye by reducing your brush size so you can be more precise.

TIP: You can adjust your brush size so it fits inside those white parts by pressing the Left and Right Bracket keys to make it smaller or larger, respectively.

Whitening Eyes.jpg @ 200% (Layer 1, RGB/8)

200%   6.833 inches x 5.125 inches (72 ppi)

Continued

STEP 5:

That's really all there is to it. Often the effect may be a little too intense but we can fix that easily since we made a duplicate of the photo in Step 2. Just drop the opacity of the top layer down to about 75% to lessen the effect. By the way, you'll often see me duplicate that Background layer throughout this book. That's a very popular way of giving yourself some wiggle room after you're done retouching, so you can bring back some of the original photo.

Before

After

I've often shown people how to change eye color in their portraits. As I was writing this book, I started thinking to myself how often that would be used. You're probably working with photos of your family or friends so wouldn't it be better if you could enhance their eye color and not change it? After all, everyone would know the eye color was changed once they met the person. Enhancing the eye color is a different story though. Here you can really make a difference to a person's portrait while still keeping their reality intact.

Enhancing
Eye Color

STEP 1:
Start out with a photo where the eye color just isn't all that catchy.

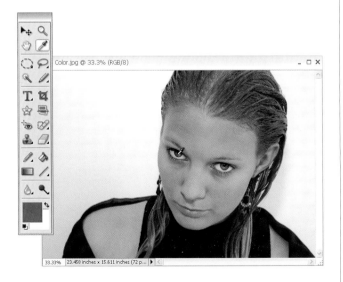

STEP 2:
Now, let's use the color of the original eye to enhance it. Choose the Eyedropper tool (I) from the Toolbox. Then, click on the iris of the eye to sample its color. If you look at the Foreground color swatch at the bottom of the Toolbox, you'll see that it shows the color you just clicked on.

Continued

STEP 3:

Click on that Foreground color swatch to open the Color Picker. Click on the S radio button on the right side of the dialog (S stands for saturation, by the way) and drag the slider, just to the left of the radio buttons, upward until it's about one-quarter of the way from the top. Now click on the B radio button and do the same. Click OK. This gives us an enhanced version of the original color to work with.

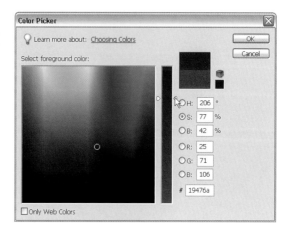

STEP 4:

Click on the Create a New Layer icon at the top of the Layers palette to create a blank layer on top of the original photo.

STEP 5:

Okay, select the Zoom tool (Z) and click-and-drag around the eyes to zoom in on them. Now select the Brush tool (FYI...the keyboard shortcut for that is B—trust me, it's a big timesaver when you're retouching photos) and choose a brush size that fits inside the iris. On the blank layer, start painting over the iris of one eye with the new color you created in Step 3. Don't worry if you go too far into a non-colored area, we can fix that in a minute. Then, move over and do the same for the other eye.

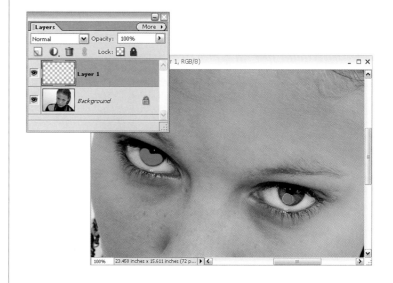

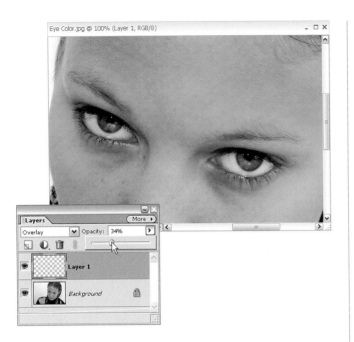

STEP 6:

If you painted over any areas in Step 5 that you didn't mean to, select the Eraser tool (E) and erase them away at this point. Finally, change the blend mode of the layer from Normal to Overlay and drop the opacity to about 30–40%. Turn the layer on and off by clicking the little Eye icon to the left of the layer thumbnail to see your before and after. Pretty cool, huh? You've actually enhanced the color by using the original color of that person's eye.

Before

After

Adding That Twinkle to the Eyes

I originally called this tutorial "Enhancing Catch Lights in Eyes." Then I sat down with a few folks to get feedback about the techniques I was including in this book, and only a few of them knew what catch lights were, so I renamed it. What we're really doing here is enhancing the catch lights in a person's eye. "What are catch lights?" is probably the next logical question. Catch lights are simply the specular highlights (really bright areas) in a person's eyes that are a result of the lighting around that person. You probably never even notice they're there, but trust me, if they weren't you'd know.

STEP 1:

Open the photo that you're going to enhance. From the Toolbox, select the Elliptical Marquee tool (press M until you have it). Drag an oval around an eye area. At this point, you don't have to be perfect, so feel free to make it larger than it needs to be. After you draw the first oval selection, press-and-hold the Shift key to add to the original selection and drag another oval around the other eye. Press Ctrl-J (Mac: Command-J) to duplicate that selection onto its own layer right above the Background layer.

STEP 2:

With your new layer selected, go to the Filter menu and choose Stylize>Emboss. Set the Angle to 135°, the Height to 2 pixels, and the Amount setting to 300%. Click OK to apply the filter. Yes, I realize the person looks like a cross between E.T. and a person from a Stephen King novel, but don't worry, we'll fix it in a minute.

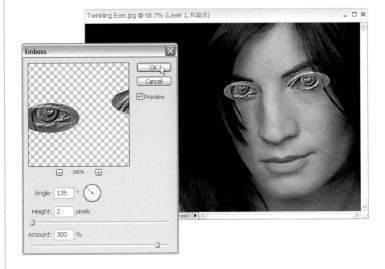

STEP 3:

Change the blend mode of that top layer to Hard Light and drop the layer's opacity down to about 60–70%. I know it looks weird, but bear with me.

STEP 4:

Press Z to get the Zoom tool, zoom way in on one eye, and select the Eraser tool (E). Use a soft-edged brush and erase away any of the unwanted areas that aren't inside the iris of the eye. Do the same for the other eye and you're done.

Continued

STEP 5:

If the effect isn't noticeable enough, go ahead and press Ctrl-J (Mac: Command-J) to duplicate the layer. Try it once again to see how much more intense the twinkle gets and even try it a third time to further intensify the effect. If you go too far, you can always delete the top layer or reduce its opacity a little.

Before

After

Here's one that can really make an impact on a photo of a person with fair skin and light hair. Often, their eyebrows will barely look noticeable because they blend in so much with their face. Eyebrows are really a distinguishing feature that will draw us into the photo, so it's important that we notice them right away as we look toward the eyes.

Darkening Eyebrows

STEP 1:

Open the photo you'll need to fix. Press Ctrl-J (Mac: Command-J) to duplicate the Background layer, so you have two image layers in the Layers palette.

STEP 2:

Select the Burn tool from the Toolbox (or press O until you have it). It's in the same place as the Dodge tool was in the "Whitening the Eyes" technique earlier in this chapter. Since the Burn tool is a brush, you can set the brush size just like any other brush. Set it to a size that fits inside the eyebrow, and set the Exposure setting in the Options Bar to about 30%.

Continued

STEP 3:

Press Z to get the Zoom tool, and zoom in on the eyebrows if necessary. Switch back to the Burn tool and start painting over one eyebrow to darken it. The more times you click and paint over an area, the more of the effect you'll apply, so be careful here. Often just once or twice over it will do just fine. Now, paint over the other eyebrow.

STEP 4:

Much like we've done in the other techniques in this chapter, drop the Opacity setting of the duplicate layer down a little. Somewhere between 70–80% works pretty good for me, but it can vary depending on just how light the eyebrows were to start with. Drop it down to 40% if they were darker in the beginning, or try 90% if they were really light to start out with.

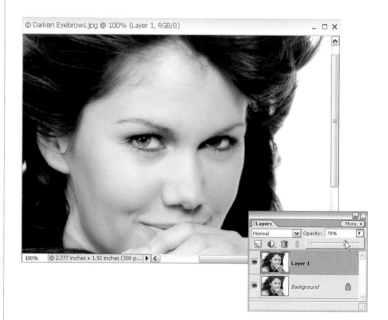

Before

After

Thickening Eyelashes

This is one of my favorite techniques. First, because it makes such an overall impact on a photo, especially if the person (most likely a woman) didn't put much (or any) eye makeup on that day, or if she just has few to no eyelashes to build up. I also love this technique because I get to use the Smudge tool, and let me tell ya, any time I get to use the Smudge tool, things are good. Okay, I'm really being sarcastic in case you haven't figured it out yet. I rarely ever use the Smudge tool for anything but it works out great for this technique.

PART 1: Thickening and Extending

This first part deals with thickening and extending the existing eyelashes. In the next part, we'll take a look at how to add some in where there may not be any.

STEP 1:

Open a photo of someone whose eyelashes need some help, and click on the Create a New Layer icon at the top of the Layers palette to create a new blank layer.

STEP 2:

Select the Smudge tool from the Toolbox (or press R until you have it). Much like the Dodge and Burn tools, it's buried near the bottom of the Toolbox in the second to last spot. Once you select the Smudge tool, turn on the Sample All Layers checkbox in the Options Bar and set the Strength to 50%.

Eyelashes.jpg @ 125% (Layer 1, RGB/8)

125%   10.444 inches x 8.861 inches (72 ppi)

STEP 3:

Click once on the blank layer to select it. Press Z to get the Zoom tool, zoom into the eye, switch back to the Smudge tool, and start painting by clicking-and-dragging along the shape of each eyelash. Start at the inside of the eye and drag outward. Remember that the Smudge tool is a brush, so you can adjust the size to suit the size of your eyelashes. Usually a very small size works best here—something around 2–4 pixels is a good size.

Eyelashes.jpg @ 100% (Layer 1, RGB/8)

Layers   More ▶
Normal   Opacity: 70%

Layer 1

Background

STEP 4:

Back in Step 2, you chose an option called Sample All Layers. By turning that option on, Elements lets you create all of the smudging and eyelash extension on a separate blank layer. This lets you drop the opacity in case you need to lessen the effect.

Continued

PART 2: Adding Eyelashes Where They Don't Exist

You've just seen how to extend eyelashes that were already there. However, if you look toward the bottom of the eye in the photo we just used, you'll see that there are barely any eyelashes there. While it's natural for them to be lighter here, you can still enhance this area to give the eye more impact. Let's take a look:

STEP 1:

Using the same photo as before, create another blank layer on top of the original photo by clicking on the Create a New Layer icon at the top of the Layers palette.

STEP 2:

Select the Brush tool (B) and choose a 1-pixel, hard-edged brush from the Brush Picker in the Options Bar. It should be the first brush in the Default Brushes set. Press D to set your Foreground and Background colors to their default settings, and start painting along the existing eyelashes to darken them. Then start creating a few in between the existing ones to thicken the area. I know, it looks pretty harsh right now but we'll fix that in the next step.

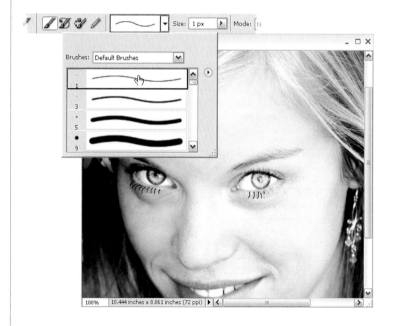

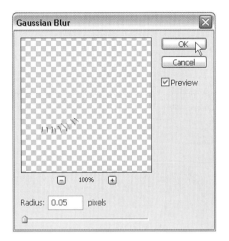

STEP 3:

After you're done painting, go to the Filter menu and select Blur>Gaussian Blur. Enter .05 for the Radius setting and click OK. This will soften the eyelashes a bit.

STEP 4:

Finally, drop the opacity of this layer to 20%, and this will significantly lighten them to make them look more realistic. However, it's going to leave just enough to enhance the overall eye.

TIP: Go ahead and try this technique on the existing eyelashes on the top of the eye. It works really well there too, if you've got some areas to fill in and darken.

Continued

Before

After

No retouching book would be complete without a tutorial on fixing red eye. In fact, we authors have a code that states that all books must contain one. Sorry, I didn't make the rule. I'm merely a pawn in this whole game, so I did what I was told. Seriously though, red eye is a very common problem when shooting in low light with an on-camera flash. Here's my suggestion: while many cameras have a red-eye reduction feature (the camera flashes several times), I'd suggest not using it, because people walk away after the first flash and ruin the photo—just fix it here. It's easy, I promise.

Fixing Red Eye

STEP 1:

Open a photo with red eye. This photo was taken with a point-and-shoot digital camera, indoors, at night. That situation is just crying for a red-eye fix.

STEP 2:

Go to the Enhance menu and choose Auto Red Eye Fix. Most of the time this will do the trick right off the bat.

Continued

STEP 3:

If that didn't do it, then select the Red Eye Removal tool (Y) from the Toolbox. The way it works is you zoom in on the eye and click on the red part, or click-and-drag a square selection around it. Like magic, the red disappears while everything else stays the same.

Before

After

I know what you're thinking already, "A tutorial on retouching pets?" You're saying to yourself, "What kind of book have I bought? A retouching book with a picture of Lassie in it?" Here's my side of the story. Pets are people too. We buy Christmas presents for them, even though they have no idea it's a holiday. Do they even know what a holiday is? Heck, we even buy health insurance for our pets and let them sleep in our beds with us. If that doesn't constitute a part of the family, then I don't know what does. So, here's a trick my buddy Larry Becker showed me in the full version of Photoshop. Fortunately, it works just as well here in Elements.

Removing Green Eye from Pets

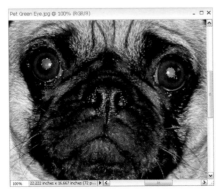

CARLINE ZUMBANO

STEP 1:
Open a photo of your favorite furry friend. I'm actually not sure whose dog this is, but I don't personally have one. Why, you ask? I have two little boys that: (a) keep us plenty busy, and (b) would take every opportunity to sit on top of whatever dog we chose and yell "Giddyup!" Trust me, you can ask our cat Jake what happens every time he inadvertently (and regrettably) strays too close to the kids.

STEP 2:
Select the Elliptical Marquee tool (press M until you have it), and click-and-drag out a circle around the green area in one of the dog's eyes. To get a circle instead of an ellipse, press-and-hold the Shift key while you drag. If you need to move the circle (or ellipse) to line it up over the pupil, press the Spacebar while you're dragging. Release the mouse button when you're done. Press-and-hold the Shift key again to add to the selection and drag another circle around the green area in the other eye, so both are now selected.

Continued

STEP 3:

Click on the little half-black/half-white circle at the top of the Layers palette (it's really called the Create Adjustment Layer icon) and choose Hue/Saturation. When the dialog opens, drag the Saturation slider all the way to the left to remove all of the color from the pupils. Click OK when you're done.

STEP 4:

Choose Select>Reselect (or press Ctrl-Shift-D [Mac: Command-Shift-D]) to re-create the same selection. This time, click on the Create Adjustment Layer icon in the Layers palette and choose Levels. When the dialog opens, drag the black Input Levels slider toward the right to darken the eyes. You'll probably need to take it about halfway across to get them all black. Click OK when you're done, and now you can not only make your people photos look great, but your pet photos too.

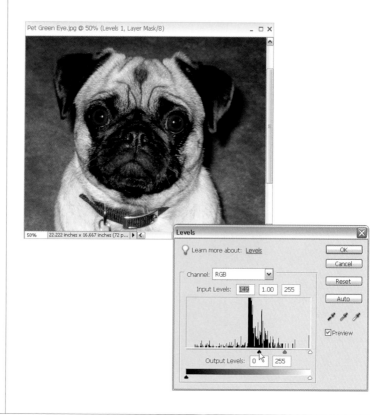

Ever look at a person without seeing their mouth and yet you can tell that they're smiling? It happens to me all the time. Our eyes can tell a great story about how we feel. However, once in a while I'll see someone with one eye that tends to squint when they smile. Typically, we don't even notice this when we're talking to them, but it really shows when you see them in photos.

Opening Squinted Eyes

STEP 1:

When you find a photo with a squinted eye, first make sure that both eyes aren't squinted. Many people's eyes squint when they smile and that's part of their character. You probably don't want to change that. However, the photo I have here shows that the man's one eye is clearly squinted more than the other.

STEP 2:

Go under the Filter menu and choose Distort>Liquify. When the Liquify dialog opens, choose the Bloat tool on the left side (it's the sixth one down, or press B to get it). Then increase or decrease the Brush Size setting until your brush appears to encompass the entire eye and even a little of the eyebrow on top of it.

Continued

STEP 3:

Once you have the tool selected and your brush the right size, position your cursor over the eye and click once. Take a look to see how much it enlarged the eye, and if it doesn't look large enough yet, then click again until the squinted eye looks more like the other one.

Before

After

Some people naturally have dark areas under their eyes. Others have them as a result of age or just plain being tired. Since the eyes tend to draw the most attention when viewing a portrait, these circles make a great candidate for retouching.

Removing Dark Circles Under Eyes

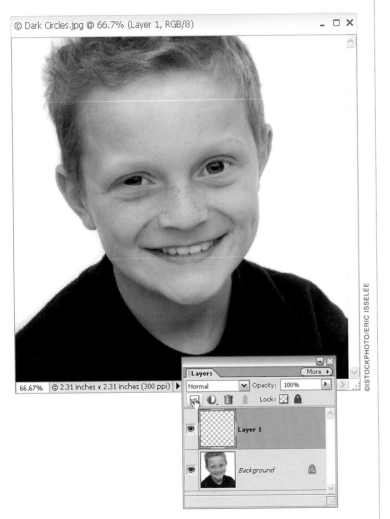

© Dark Circles.jpg @ 66.7% (Layer 1, RGB/8)

66.67%   © 2.31 inches x 2.31 inches (300 ppi)

©ISTOCKPHOTO/ERIC ISSELÉE

Layers   More ►

Normal   Opacity: 100%

Lock:

Layer 1

Background

STEP 1:
Start out with a photo that has dark circles under the eyes. At this point, you should start learning the drill, but in case you haven't, let's go ahead and create a brand new blank layer by clicking on the Create a New Layer icon at the top of the Layers palette. This will let us do our retouching on a blank layer and blend it in with the original skin.

Continued

STEP 2:

Select the Healing Brush tool from the Toolbox (or press J until you have it). Then make sure the Sample All Layers checkbox is turned on up in the Options Bar. Finally, lower your brush's Hardness setting in the Brush Picker, and choose a size that is slightly larger than the circles you plan on fixing here.

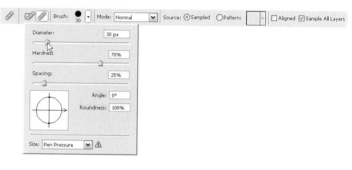

STEP 3:

The Healing Brush works by first selecting a clean sample area to work. We do this by pressing-and-holding the Alt (Mac: Option) key and clicking in a nicely textured area of the face (preferably near or below the eye itself so the skin color and tone are the same).

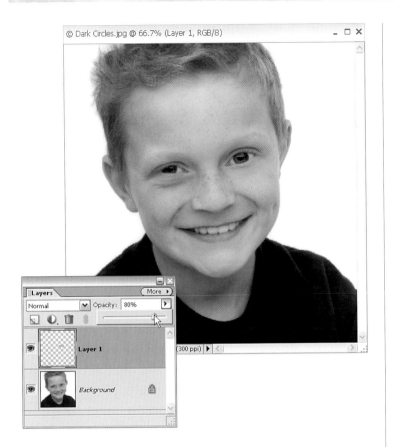

© Dark Circles.jpg @ 66.7% (Layer 1, RGB/8)

Layers   More ▶
Normal   Opacity: 80%
Layer 1
Background

(300 ppi)

STEP 4:

Now that we have our source, click once on the blank layer to select it and start painting over the dark circles in your image. When you release your mouse, the Healing Brush will meld the sampled area in with the area you just painted over and smooth everything out. Notice how it keeps much of the texture and skin tone intact and just removes the dark areas? Also, don't forget that we did the retouching on a blank layer so you can always drop the opacity of that layer to show some of the original skin texture and color. I usually drop mine down to about 80%.

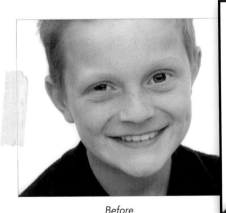

Before

After

Removing Glare from Glasses

This tutorial is here by popular request. Just about everyone I polled when I asked what type of things they wanted to learn from this book said that they needed to remove glare and reflections from glasses. Even as popular as those anti-reflective coatings have gotten, you'll still find people that don't have it. Again, it's one of those things that you're probably not paying too much attention to when you're taking the photo, but later on, believe me, you'll see it.

METHOD 1: Overall Glare

Use this technique if your photo is easy to work with and there is a reflection over all of the glass in the glasses.

STEP 1:

Here I've got a photo that has an even reflection over all of the glass in the glasses. If you get this then you're in luck, because it's fairly simple to fix. The next method that I'll show you is a bit more involved.

STEP 2:

First, we need to make a selection of the inside of the glasses. I like the Selection Brush for this, so get that tool from the Toolbox (it is nested with the Magic Selection Brush, or just press A to get it). Now, the Selection Brush works just like a regular brush does—you paint with it by clicking-and-dragging with your mouse. Each brush stroke creates a selection. Go ahead and start painting inside the glasses here to select them.

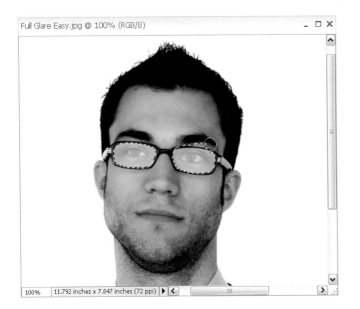

100% 11.792 inches x 7.847 inches (72 ppi)

STEP 3:

If you've accidentally gone outside the glasses when brushing, just press-and-hold the Alt (Mac: Option) key and paint over those areas to remove them from the selection.

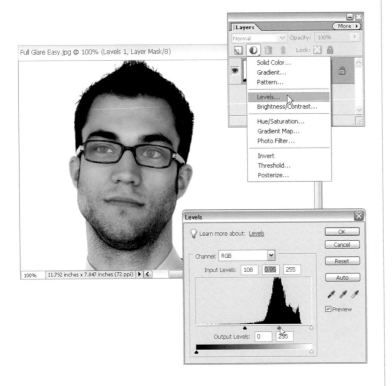

Full Glare Easy.jpg @ 100% (Levels 1, Layer Mask/8)

100% 11.792 inches x 7.847 inches (72 ppi)

STEP 4:

Once the selection is made, go to the top of the Layers palette and click on the Create Adjustment Layer icon, and then choose Levels. When the Levels dialog opens, drag the black point slider on the left over toward the right until the area inside the glasses begins to match the area around them. If you can't get it perfect, try dragging the middle (midtones) slider to the left or right a little and that should get you there. Click OK and you're done.

Continued

It's All in the Eyes   Chapter 2   47

METHOD 2: Random Glare

Use this method if you're not so lucky and the glare is randomly spread throughout the glasses.

STEP 1:

Once you open the photo with glare, I suggest you come up with a game plan. Fixing random glare like this can be tricky, so here's what I do: I pick the eye that looks better and I fix it first. Which eye is better? Well, I look for areas that are easy to replace. For example, the eye on the right side has some serious glare below the eyeball itself. However, the area surrounding it is all skin. Skin is fairly easy to replace since I can use the clean skin area to replace the skin with glare on it. Now, the eye on the left side has a lot more glare over the color and white part of the eye itself. There really isn't area around it that is smooth and easy to sample from, so that side would be harder to replace in my opinion. So, I've decided to work with the eye on the right side first. If we're lucky, we can use it to help us with the eye on the left.

STEP 2:

The first thing to do is click on the Create a New Layer icon at the top of the Layers palette to create a new blank layer. This will help us separate our work so we can use it later to help with the other eye.

STEP 3:

Select the Healing Brush tool (press J until you have it) and make sure you turn on the Sample All Layers checkbox in the Options Bar at the top. Make sure the blank layer is selected in the Layers palette so all of our changes happen there. Now press-and-hold the Alt (Mac: Option) key and sample an area toward the area without glare near the nose.

STEP 4:

Start painting, with a 15-pixel brush for this photo, from the inside toward the outside of the glasses to smooth the area below the eye. Use a few quick, small brush strokes and work your way from the inside toward the outside.

STEP 5:

Now select the Clone Stamp tool (S) from the Toolbox. Again, make sure the Sample All Layers checkbox is turned on up in the Options Bar. Press-and-hold the Alt (Mac: Option) key to sample an area near the glare at the top-right side of the eye to start removing that large white glare.

Continued

STEP 6:

Using the Zoom tool (Z), zoom in closer on the eye. Paint with the Clone Stamp tool, using a soft-edged brush, to start removing that white glare right below the top of the frames. Try not to go into the eyelashes too much at this point though. Don't forget to resize your brush as you get closer to the point where the eyelashes meet the frames.

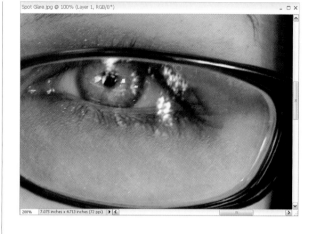

STEP 7:

Now, press-and hold the Alt (Mac: Option) key and sample an area in the eyelashes of the same eye.

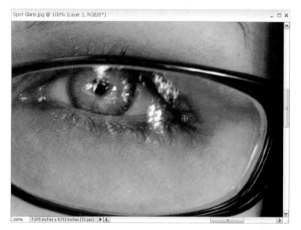

STEP 8:

Start painting with quick, small strokes again to paint away the glare over the eyelashes. Start on the inside near the white part of the eye and paint outward to the frames. Again, make sure you use several brush strokes and resample by pressing-and-holding the Alt (Mac: Option) key often to avoid noticeable patterns.

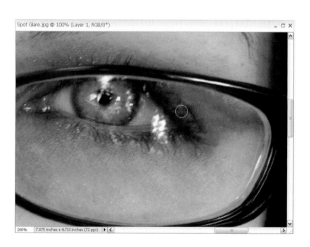

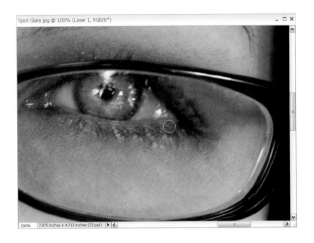

STEP 9:

Use the same method in Steps 7 and 8 to remove the glare from the eyelashes at the bottom of the eye. Make sure you sample an area with the Clone Stamp tool that is under the eye because the eyelashes are now going in a different direction.

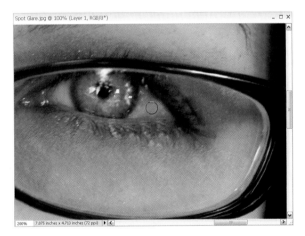

STEP 10:

Next, use the Clone Stamp tool to remove the glare over the white area of the eye. Again, sample a nearby area to make sure the tone matches. Be careful not to flow into the colored area or the eyelashes though.

STEP 11:

Continue using the Clone Stamp tool to remove the white glare from the colored parts of the eye. Some of the white parts are part of the catch lights (twinkle areas) in the eye, so don't feel the need to get rid of every last speck of white.

Continued

STEP 12:

Whew! I know that part was a lot of work, but we've actually got the hard part done at this point. The rest is pretty easy (well, maybe, that is). Here's the thing: In this photo, I'm going to duplicate the eye we just fixed and use it to replace the eye on the other side. It works great here because of the way the woman is facing. However, if you're not so lucky after you try this method, then you'll probably have to work on the other eye just like we did the first one. It's a little more work I know, but getting rid of this much glare just ain't that simple.

We're going to duplicate the right eye and move it over the left one to make the repair much easier.

STEP 13:

Double-click the Zoom tool in the Toolbox to zoom out so you can see the whole photo again. Select the Elliptical Marquee tool from the Toolbox (or press M until you have it) and draw an ellipse over the right eye that we just fixed.

STEP 14:

You may have never actually seen this command before, but go under the Edit menu and choose Copy Merged (Ctrl-Shift-C [Mac: Command-Shift-C]). This not only copies the contents of the layer you have selected in the Layers palette but it copies everything within the selection—regardless of what layer it's on.

STEP 15:

Now choose Edit>Paste or just press Ctrl-V (Mac: Command-V) to Paste the copied eye onto its own layer. You may want to double-click on the name of this layer in the Layers palette and rename it "Left Eye" to help yourself keep track of it.

STEP 16:

Go under the Image menu and choose Rotate>Flip Layer Horizontal so the eye will fit on the other side of the face. Then select the Move tool (V) and move the duplicate eye to the left, over the original.

STEP 17:

Decrease the Opacity setting of the Left Eye layer to 50% so we can see what's under it. Then press Ctrl-T (Mac: Command-T) to enter Free Transform mode.

Continued

STEP 18:

Position your cursor outside the bounding box that appears. You'll see that it turns into a rounded, two-headed arrow. Click-and-drag to rotate the eye so it matches up as closely as possible with the original one below it. Keep an eye on the pupil as a good reference. Match that area up first with the one below it and then try to get the angle correct. You can always put your cursor inside the box and click-and-drag to move the eye in a straight line for a better fit. Once you're happy with the match, press the Enter (Mac: Return) key to commit the transformation.

STEP 19:

We're almost there. You've got the eye in place and the glare is gone. The only thing left to do is get rid of the areas around the eye that don't belong. Return the opacity of the Left Eye layer to 100%. Then select the Eraser tool (E) from the Toolbox and set your brush size to a smaller soft-edged brush (I used a 50-pixel brush here). Start erasing everything around the frame that doesn't belong so only the glare-free area inside the frame is left, and you're done. It really is that simple and only takes nearly 20 steps. Okay, I realize it was a long one but the results are pretty staggering when you think about what we started with.

Before

After

CLASS *of* 2006

Remove Braces

Chapter 3

Retouching the Mouth

After the eyes, the mouth and the smile tend to be the other areas we look at the most in a portrait. Unfortunately, there's a ton of things that can distract us in, on, or around the mouth. Teeth, lip color, braces, the overall smile…these are all things that can make or break a photo. In this chapter, we'll look at some small and subtle ways to make the entire mouth area the star of your photos.

Making Teeth Whiter

This is one of those questions that I get just about every other day. The actual form of the question ranges anywhere from "How do I get rid of yellow teeth?" to the simple, "How do I make teeth whiter?" Fortunately, the answer is just about the same for all circumstances.

METHOD 1: Brightening Dull Teeth

This one works best as an overall teeth-brightening technique. It's great for teeth that have a grayish tint to them and appear to be a little darker, but not yellow. It also works great when you just want to make the teeth pop out a little more. You can skip to Method 2 if you want to whiten yellow teeth.

STEP 1:

Open a photo where the person's teeth have a grayish darker tint to them.

STEP 2:

Add a new Levels adjustment layer by clicking on the Create Adjustment Layer icon at the top of the Layers palette and selecting Levels. When the Levels dialog opens, drag the white Input Levels slider on the right about 25% toward the left. Click OK. This will, in effect, lighten the entire photo.

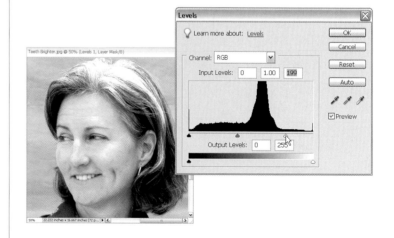

STEP 3:

After you make the adjustment, the Levels adjustment layer will appear above your photo in the Layers palette. You'll see a little white thumbnail to the right of it. It's called a mask, but don't get caught up in the name right now if you've never used one before. All you need to do is fill this thumbnail (aka: mask) with black. The easiest way is to press D, then X to set your Foreground color to black, then press Alt-Backspace (Mac: Option-Delete). This will fill the mask with black and hide the effects of the Levels adjustment that we just made.

STEP 4:

Use the Zoom tool (Z) to zoom in on the teeth if you need to. Then, press B to choose the Brush tool, press X to set your Foreground color to white, and start painting over the teeth. This will reveal the Levels adjustment on the teeth only, thus making them whiter.

TIP: If the teeth end up being too white or too dark, you can always double-click on the Levels adjustment layer's thumbnail and tweak the effect one way or the other by moving the white Input Levels slider.

Continued

Before

After

METHOD 2: Whitening Yellow Teeth

While the previous technique worked for overall teeth brightening, it would most likely just turn yellow teeth into bright yellow teeth. That's where this technique steps in. It works best on teeth that have a yellow tint to them.

STEP 1:

Open a photo where the person's teeth appear to have a yellow tint.

Teeth Whiter.jpg @ 50% (RGB/8)

50%

©FOTOLIA/B. SILVA

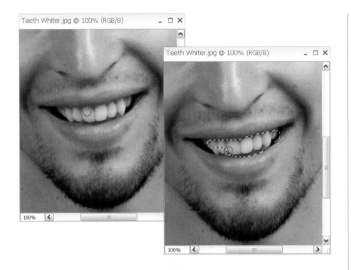

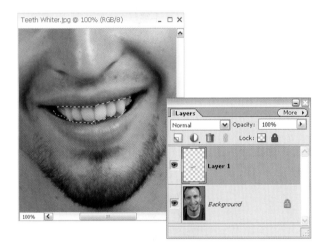

STEP 2:
Press Z to get the Zoom tool and zoom in on the teeth. Press A to get the Selection Brush. Then, in the Options Bar, choose a soft-edged brush from the Brush Picker that is about half the size of one of the teeth.

STEP 3:
Start painting with the Selection Brush to select the teeth. I do a quick pass over the edges first. Then click-and-paint again to cover the rest of the area. Don't worry if you select a part of the surrounding area, though. We'll fix that in the next step.

TIP: Remember that the Selection Brush is just like any other brush. You can always resize your brush using the Left and Right Bracket keys. That will help you get into those hard-to-reach areas.

STEP 4:
If you've inadvertently painted over some other areas (lips, gums, etc.), then press-and-hold the Alt (Mac: Option) key and start painting to remove them.

STEP 5:
Once you've got the teeth selected, press Ctrl-J (Mac: Command-J) to copy them onto a new layer.

STEP 6:
Now go to the Enhance menu and choose Adjust Color>Replace Color.

Continued

STEP 7:

In the Replace Color dialog, drag the Fuzziness slider all the way to the right to 200. Then at the bottom of the dialog, take the Saturation slider and move it to the left to around -40. Then take the Lightness slider and move it to the right to +15–20. Try 20 first, and if it's too bright then pull back to 15. Click OK and you're done. The teeth should be nice and white.

Before

After

I debated whether or not I should call this tutorial "Luscious Lips," but I thought better of it. This technique is great for giving the lips just a little extra punch. Here, we'll enhance the color of the lips. Often, you'll find that the lip color is just too lifeless, but there's an easy way to fix that.

Enhancing the Lips

©FOTOLIA/NADEZDA ISAEVA

STEP 1:
Open the photo where the subject's lips look like they blend in with everything else on the face.

STEP 2:
Click on the Create Adjustment Layer icon at the top of the Layers palette and select Hue/Saturation. When the Hue/Saturation dialog opens, the Edit pop-up menu at the top should read Master. Go ahead and change this to Reds because we want to target the red tones directly here.

Continued

STEP 3:

Drag the Saturation slider over toward the right until you start to see the lips turn redder. Don't go too far just yet because you don't want that drastic of a change. Somewhere around +15–20 is good to start with. Click OK to close the dialog.

STEP 4:

In making this adjustment, you've really enhanced all of the reds in the photo which is not what we're after. So, let's restrict it to just the lips. Press D, then X to set your Foreground color to black, then click once on the Hue/Saturation adjustment layer's mask to select it, and fill it with black by pressing Alt-Backspace (Mac: Option-Delete). Doing this hides the red-enhancing effect we just created.

STEP 5:

Now press B to choose the Brush tool, press X to set your Foreground color to white, and start painting over the lips. You'll start to see the red re-appear back in the lips but not the rest of the photo. If you mess up and paint too far, just press X again to switch your Foreground color back to black and paint it away. Now you can double-click on the Hue/Saturation adjustment layer to tweak the red color to make it stronger or weaker. This way you'll only see it on the lips and not the rest of the photo.

Before

After

Make 'em Smile

What is it about smiling? Some people can't wait to get in front of the camera and will show us those pearly whites without hesitation. Others just refuse to smile. It happens a lot with kids and pre-teens. They seem to hit a point where it's not "cool" to smile. Little do they know that you have Photoshop Elements, though. In addition to the multitude of embarrassing things you can do to a person, with a few clicks of the mouse you can at least add a little smirk to those that won't smile for the camera.

STEP 1:

Find a photo of that person that just won't smile for you. Now it's time for revenge. Well, kind of—we really can't add teeth in there, but at least we can make them look somewhat happy.

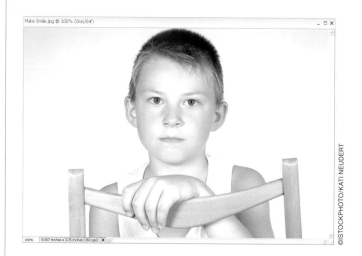

STEP 2:

Go to the Filter menu and choose Distort>Liquify. Press W to select the Warp tool (it's the first tool at the top left). In the Tool Options on the right side of the dialog, increase your brush size until your brush is roughly the size of half the mouth.

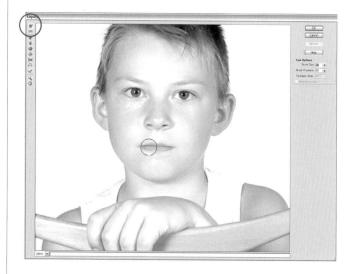

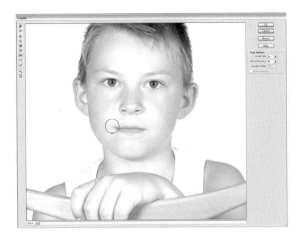

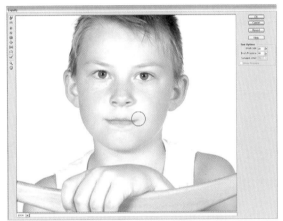

STEP 3:

Making a person smile isn't as much about the mouth as it is the cheek area around it. If you were to just curl the mouth upward, it would look kind of funny. Instead, it's the muscles in the cheek area that seem to pull the lips upward. So, put only about a quarter of your brush over the edge of the mouth and leave the rest of it above and outside in the cheek area. Then simply click-and-drag upward to add a little smile to those frowning lips.

STEP 4:

Switch over and do the other side. If you find the effect is too much and you're having a hard time keeping it from looking fake, then try dropping the Brush Pressure setting on the right side of the dialog. This will give you a little more room for error.

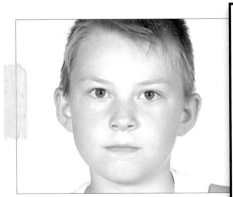

Before

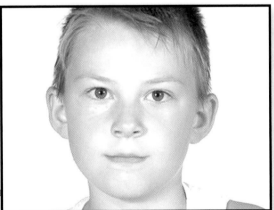

After

Fixing Spaces Between Teeth

Some folks are blessed with perfect teeth. Others (myself included) are not so blessed. Most of the time it's okay, but once in a while a space between the teeth may be a little distracting to the overall photo. Luckily we have Elements to fix this. Be careful though, you don't want to hurt your subject's feelings by making them think they had all of these problems. Remember, they're going to see the portrait you're creating. Make it real by doing selective and tasteful work—not a total makeover.

STEP 1:

After you locate the photo with the space between the teeth that you'd like to fix, go ahead and create a blank layer on top of it (by clicking on the Create a New Layer icon at the top of the Layers palette). We're going to use the Clone Stamp tool here, so we might as well take advantage of the fact that it'll let us work on a blank layer.

©FOTOLIA/PHILIP DATE

STEP 2:

Press Z to zoom into the photo and then select the Clone Stamp tool from the Toolbox (or just press the letter S). In the Options Bar, turn on the Sample All Layers checkbox. What we want to do here is just extend the tooth to the side of the space a little, so we need to lower our brush size significantly so we can be precise. Press-and-hold the Alt (Mac: Option) key and sample an area right at the center and bottom of the tooth.

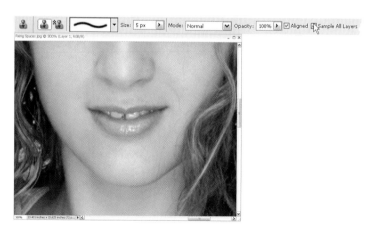

STEP 3:

Move your cursor over until it's right inside the gap (on the tooth's side). Click-and-drag from the bottom part of the tooth and follow the contour of it as it moves up toward the lip or gum. You're essentially extending the side of the tooth here.

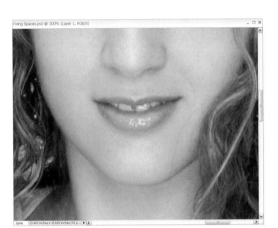

STEP 4:

Depending on the gap, you may be able to get away with one brush stroke here. If not, resample and continue extending the tooth until the gap is closed.

Before

After

Fixing Crooked Teeth

Just like the technique before this one, fixing teeth is a tricky thing. There's a fine line between offending the subject and a tasteful enhancement. A good rule of thumb here is to not make any adjustments to other people that you wouldn't do to yourself. Here, we have a nice photo of a couple, and with one small adjustment to the teeth we can really make the smile stand out.

STEP 1:

Open the photo that you're going to fix. Start out by creating a blank layer above the Background layer by clicking on the Create a New Layer icon at the top of the Layers palette.

STEP 2:

Click once on the blank layer to select it, press the letter Z to get the Zoom tool, and zoom in on the teeth. Then press S to select the Clone Stamp tool and make sure that the Sample All Layers checkbox is turned on in the Options Bar. Press-and-hold the Alt (Mac: Option) key and click on the top of the space between two other teeth to sample that area. The best way to fix crooked teeth is by building a straight space between the teeth that need fixing.

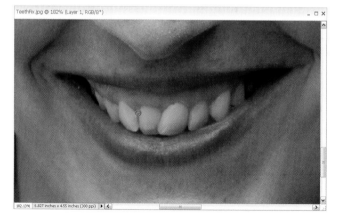

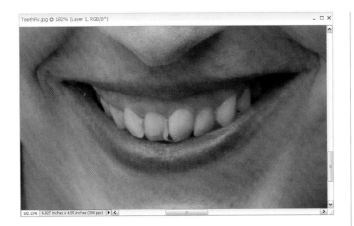

STEP 3:
Now, with the Clone Stamp tool, paint straight down the center of the two middle teeth to build a fake space between them. As you get toward the bottom, start curving the brush stroke along the contour of the tooth.

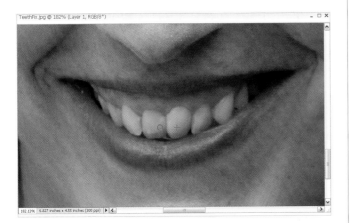

STEP 4:
Press-and-hold the Alt (Mac: Option) key again and sample the center of the tooth on the right. Then click-and-drag to start painting on the tooth on the left to get rid of the part of the original tooth we left behind in the last step.

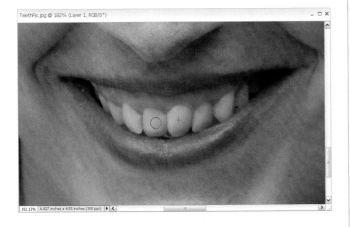

STEP 5:
You may need to do this a few times to get the teeth to match up. Continually resample with the Clone Stamp tool to keep patterns from starting to appear.

Continued

STEP 6:

The last thing to do is to fix the area of space between the lip and the teeth. Zoom in on that area and you'll see some remnants of the tooth shape that was originally there.

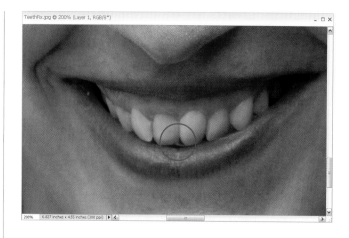

STEP 7:

Now, select the Eyedropper tool (I) and click on a dark spot in that empty area to sample the color. (You'll see your sampled color in your Foreground color swatch at the bottom of the Toolbox.)

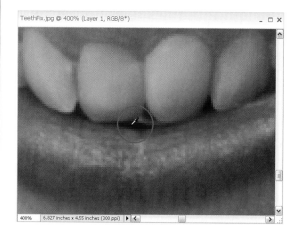

STEP 8:

Switch to the Brush tool (B) and drop your brush size way down until it fits inside this area. Start painting over the ghosted tooth shape to remove it and restore a realistic appearance between the teeth and the lip below them.

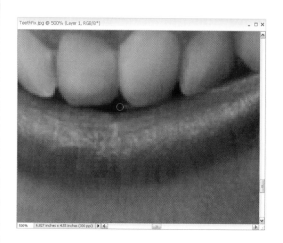

Before

After

Removing Braces

Remember how I said there's a fine line between tasteful retouching and retouching that is just flat-out fake? Well, in this tutorial we're going to make an exception because braces aren't really a part of anyone's life that they care to remember. They're not part of us. They're a temporary fix for something and most people can't wait to get them off, so it's okay to take a creative approach here—especially if it's a portrait that you're going to look back on one day. Why remember the braces—just remember the smile.

WARNING: Before we begin, I have to warn you that this is a fairly advanced tutorial. Braces are a very invasive thing when it comes to teeth and they don't leave much of the original tooth exposed. Because of this, it takes some serious time and effort to remove them. Sorry, I don't want to scare you away. I just want to let you know this one may take some extra time. As a reference, it took me about 30–45 minutes to work on the image in this tutorial.

STEP 1:
Open a photo of someone with braces. If you're lucky, they have those newer braces that are transparent or the color of teeth. If not, they're the silver kind. As you can see here in this photo, we're working with the old silver kind.

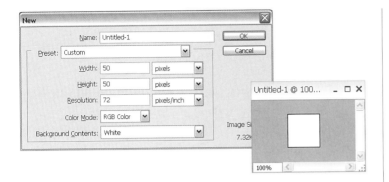

STEP 2:

The first part is something I learned from Jane Conner-Ziser and it's a great little trick. First, choose File>New>Blank File and create a new document. Enter 50 pixels for the Width and Height, 72 ppi for Resolution, and choose RGB Color as the Color Mode. Click OK to make the document.

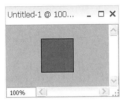

STEP 3:

Choose Edit>Fill Layer to open the Fill Layer dialog. Change the Use setting to 50% Gray and hit OK. This fills the layer with a neutral gray color.

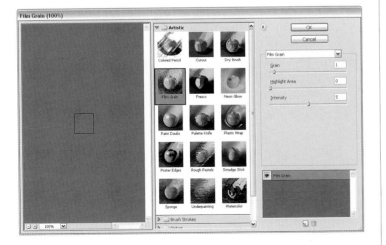

STEP 4:

Now choose Filter>Artistic>Film Grain. Set the Grain to 1, the Highlight Area to 0, and the Intensity to 5, then hit OK.

Continued

STEP 5:

Press Ctrl-A (Mac: Command-A) to Select All. Go to the Edit menu and choose Define Pattern from Selection. In the Pattern Name dialog, give your pattern a descriptive name like "Removing Braces Pattern" and click OK.

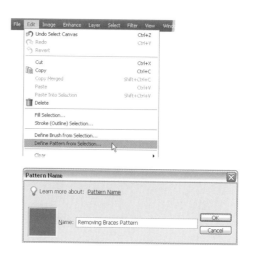

STEP 6:

Okay, we've just created a pattern that is going to help us remove the braces. Now it's time to remove them. Switch back to your photo and press the letter Z to get the Zoom tool and zoom in on the braces. Then select the Healing Brush tool from the Toolbox (or press J until you have it). In the Options Bar, set the Mode to Screen and click on the Pattern radio button. Then click the small down-facing arrow next to the Pattern thumbnail and from the Pattern Picker, click on the pattern that you just saved in Step 5. Don't forget to turn on the Sample All Layers checkbox.

STEP 7:

Also in the Options Bar, set the Healing Brush to a soft-edged brush in a size that is just larger than one of the braces. Click on the Create a New Layer icon at the top of the Layers palette to create a new blank layer. Then, click in the center of one of the braces to start removing it. As you click, you'll see it start to disappear. Click a few more times until it's gone. Don't worry that the wire is still there—we'll take care of that in another step. Right now, we're just going to get rid of the big areas.

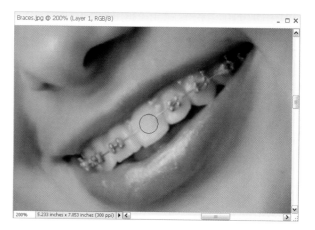

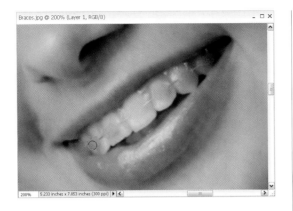

STEP 8:

Do the same for the rest of the braces on the teeth. Make sure you change the brush size to take into account the teeth that are receding into the background. The closer you keep your brush strokes over only the braces, the better things will turn out. Use the shortcut Ctrl-[(Left Bracket; Mac: Command-[) to increase the brush size or Ctrl-] (Right Bracket; Mac: Command-]) to decrease it.

STEP 9:

Now, decrease your brush size so it's just slightly larger than the wire. Click on the wire with the Healing Brush and start removing it just like you did the braces.

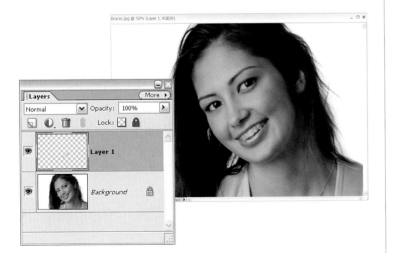

STEP 10:

Okay, we've got a good start here and we've done a lot of the heavy work. Now it's time to take care of the details. At this point, your image should look similar to mine and your Layers palette should have just two layers—the original photo and the layer on top that we've been doing all of our healing work on.

Continued

STEP 11:

The first thing we need to do is add some spaces between the teeth. They all seem to blend together at this point. Select the Eyedropper tool (I) and click to sample the color between two of the teeth where a space is still intact. This will change your Foreground color to that color you just sampled.

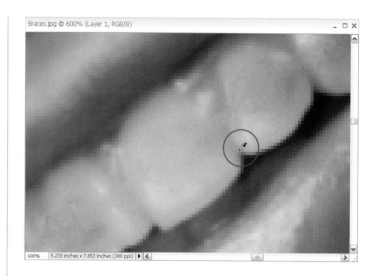

STEP 12:

Select the Brush tool (B), and choose a very small soft-edged brush—about 2–4 pixels should do. In the Options Bar, drop the Opacity of the brush down to 30%. Click on the Create a New Layer icon at the top of the Layers palette and start painting a space between those two teeth. (Double-click on the new layer's name if you want to rename it so you know what is on each layer.) Make sure you build up each paint stroke by painting over it several times, since your brush opacity is so low.

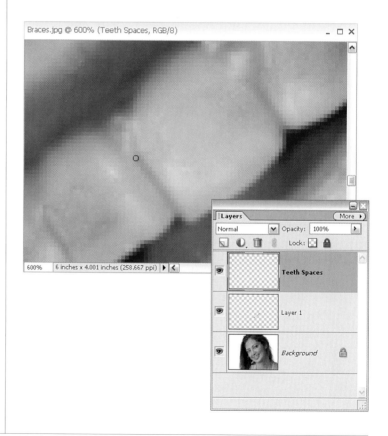

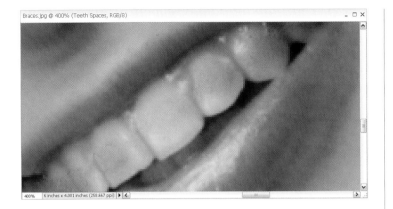

STEP 13:

Repeat Steps 11 and 12 for the spaces between each tooth. It's best to continually resample an area from the existing space between the teeth because the color changes between each one.

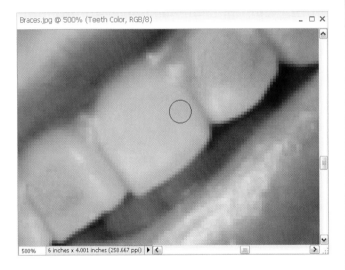

STEP 14:

Now that we've made a good start in rebuilding the teeth, it's time to start getting the color back. Create another blank layer on top of the rest. Use the Eyedropper tool to sample a color toward the center of one of the teeth, but make sure it's not over an area we healed with the Healing Brush back in Step 7. Select the Brush tool, set its opacity to 40%, and start painting on the tooth that you just sampled from (increase your brush size if needed). Again, click multiple times with the Brush tool to build up the effect.

Continued

STEP 15:

Repeat the previous step for each tooth. Because of shadows, highlights, and lighting, each tooth may be a slightly different color so make sure you sample a color from each tooth. When you get to the edges you're going to have to, well, fake it. You can probably tell that those areas are pretty much gone so you'll have to use the color from the tooth closest to it to just fill in that space. Make sure you don't go over the lips though.

STEP 16:

Whew! We're almost there. The last thing we need to do is to apply some final touches. Start out by creating a flattened version of your photo with all of the layers compressed. Since we don't want to lose the original work, in case we need to tweak it, there's a cool keyboard shortcut for this. Click once on the topmost layer to select it, and then press Ctrl-Alt-Shift-E (Mac: Command-Option-Shift-E; also known as the entire keyboard). Seriously though, this is a great shortcut and it creates one flattened layer on top of the rest.

Braces.jpg @ 50% (Layer 2, RGB/8)

50%   6 inches x 4.001 inches (258.667 ppi)

STEP 17:

Finally, select the Dodge tool from the Toolbox (or press the letter O until you have it) and set the Exposure setting in the Options Bar to 20%. Paint over the middle teeth to lighten them a bit. If needed, select the Burn tool (press the letter O again, until you have it) and do the same for the teeth on the edges to darken them a bit if they're too light. You can always look at your original photo to see the lighting and determine if the outer teeth are darker than the ones in the center.

Before

After

Crop and draw
focus to face

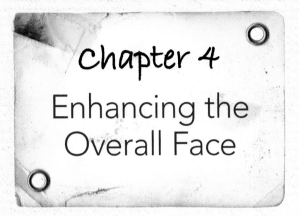

Chapter 4
Enhancing the Overall Face

Here's where we take a look at putting the finishing touches on the photo. At this point, the eyes should sparkle and the teeth and mouth should look great. Now it's time to look at the overall face. In this chapter we'll look at everything from retouching skin and wrinkles to removing blemishes.

We'll also look at the lighting on the face and see some ways to enhance it to bring out that studio quality. Finally, you'll learn some cropping techniques (specifically why, where, and how to crop portraits) to really make your portraits look their best.

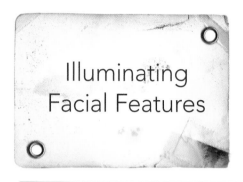

Illuminating Facial Features

When I'm taking photos, one thing I always try to do is make sure my subject is not only in focus but that I frame the shot to draw attention to the areas I want to. Part of that process deals with lighting—you always want to make sure your subject is well lit. However, it's not always possible to get the lighting you want. That's when I turn to this trick and I paint light in certain areas after the fact. It's one of my favorite techniques.

STEP 1:

Open a photo where the person or people in the photo could use a bit more lighting on them. Remember, these techniques work great for taking an already good photo and making it look great. It's always much more difficult to take a badly lit photo and make it look good, so always try to light the photo the right way when you're taking the shot.

©ISTOCKPHOTO/MATTHEW GOUGH

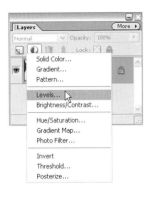

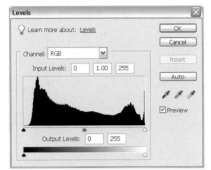

STEP 2:

Go to the top of the Layers palette and click on the Create Adjustment Layer icon. Choose Levels from the pop-up menu, and the Levels dialog will open.

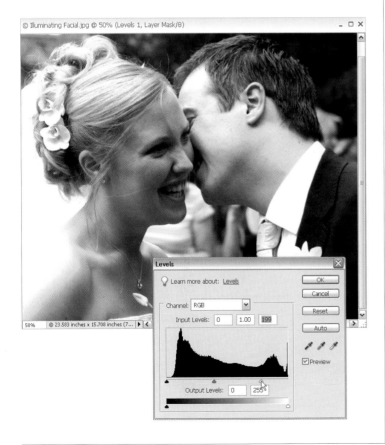

STEP 3:

Drag the white Input Levels slider on the right toward the left. How far? I really don't know yet and you probably won't either but that's okay. Just drag it far enough that the overall brightness of the people's faces increases enough that you can see it. We can tweak it later. Click OK when you're done.

Continued

STEP 4:

Notice the new adjustment layer that was added to the Layers palette? Press Ctrl-Backspace (Mac: Command-Delete) to fill the adjustment layer mask with black (your Foreground and Background colors are automatically set to white and black when the adjustment layer is added). This will hide the effects of the adjustment layer and just show the original photo—almost as if we haven't done anything yet.

STEP 5:

Now, press B to select the Brush tool. In the Options Bar, set the Opacity to 50%. With your Foreground color set to white (it should already be white if you followed the previous step), use a soft-edged brush and paint over the features that you'd like to draw attention to. This will bring back that lightening effect that we added in Step 3, but only in the areas we paint. Here, I'm mainly sticking with the main facial features (eyes, nose, mouth). I also painted over the hair to make it pop out a little more. Since your brush opacity is set to 50%, you can build up the lightening by painting back over areas that need more.

STEP 6:

Remember back in Step 3 when I said we could tweak the lighting effect later? Well it's actually really simple. Just double-click on the Levels adjustment layer thumbnail in the Layers palette to bring up the same Levels dialog. Then drag the white Input Levels slider further to the left to lighten more or to the right to darken the effect. Either way, keep your eye on the photo and what you see is what you get.

Before

After

Softening
Skin

People naturally have a texture to their skin. Some textures show up more than others and some textures are accentuated by the use of makeup. This tutorial is a great technique for simply softening those textures so the skin looks more natural.

STEP 1:

Open a photo in which you'd like to soften the skin texture on the face. As I mentioned in the opening to this tutorial, you'll often find that makeup can show up as too textured, especially when under the right light, as in this photo.

STEP 2:

Duplicate the Background layer by pressing Ctrl-J (Mac: Command-J). At this point, you should have two copies of the photo in your Layers palette (the Background layer and Layer 1).

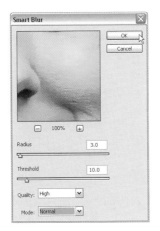

STEP 3:

Click on the top copy of the photo in the Layers palette to select it. Then go to the Filter menu and choose Blur>Smart Blur. Enter 3 for the Radius, 10 for the Threshold, and set the Quality to High. While I'm on the quality topic, have you ever wondered why there is a Low Quality setting? Seriously, when do you want to apply a Low Quality setting to your photo? It's like saying, "Yes, I want this photo to look worse." Don't get me started. Anyway, back to the matter at hand. Go ahead and set the Mode setting to Normal and click OK. This will blur the top copy of the photo. But this isn't just any blur. Remember, it's a Smart Blur. That means that Elements tries its best to keep the details in your photo intact while only blurring the smooth open surface areas.

STEP 4:

Now select the Eraser tool (E) and erase away everything, except the skin areas that you want to smooth, from the top blurred copy of the photo. This will show the sharp detailed areas in the photo underneath. That way, only the skin is softened and not everything else.

Before

After

Reducing Shiny Skin

Without getting too descriptive, our skin produces oils that cause a shine sometimes. For some people, it happens more than for others. I happen to have a high forehead for example, and my skin is always shining up there. It also happens on the cheeks and the nose. If we remove it totally, then it looks rather fake, but there's a quick fix we can do to at least soften the effect a bit.

STEP 1:

Once you find a photo of a person with shiny skin, click on the Create a New Layer icon at the top of the Layers palette to create a blank layer above the Background layer.

STEP 2:

Press S to select the Clone Stamp tool. Then in the Options Bar, enter the following settings:

Mode: Darken
Opacity: 30%
Aligned: checked
Sample All Layers: checked

Reducing Shiny Skin.jpg @ 100% (Layer 1, RGB/8)

100%   23.431 inches x 15.625 inches (72 p...

STEP 3:

Now, let's fix the nose shine first. Press Z and click in the nose area to zoom in on it, then press S again to go back to the Clone Stamp tool. From the Brush Picker in the Options Bar, select a soft-edged brush that is around the size of the small shiny areas you need to fix on the nose. With the new blank layer selected, press-and-hold the Alt (Mac: Option) key and click in a non-shiny area to sample the skin color.

Reducing Shiny Skin.jpg @ 100% (Layer 1, RGB/8)

100%   23.431 inches x 15.625 inches (72 p...

STEP 4:

Now, start painting on the problem areas to remove the shine. Don't forget to watch the little plus-sign cursor that is showing you where your sample is coming from. If it starts moving over other features of the face, you may get some unwanted results. If that happens, just press Ctrl-Z (Mac: Command-Z) to Undo and try it again with smaller brush strokes.

Continued

Enhancing the Overall Face   Chapter 4   91

STEP 5:

Now move over to the larger areas and follow the same process. First, press-and-hold the Alt (Mac: Option) key to sample the skin area around a shiny spot. Press the Right Bracket key (]) to increase your brush size because you'll have a larger area to paint. Then paint with the Clone Stamp tool over the shiny areas to reduce them.

Reducing Shiny Skin.jpg @ 100% (Layer 1, RGB/8)

100%   23.431 inches x 15.625 inches (72 p...

Before

After

There are plenty of skin conditions that can take away from the impact of your portraits. By removing them, it's not that we want to cheat reality, it's just that we want people to focus on the person in the photo—not some blemishes, freckles, or acne that may be present on their face at the time. Plus, many of these skin issues aren't even permanent. You can bet that the day it's time to wake up and pose for that portrait, there's going to be a nice pimple or blemish smack in the middle of your face for the occasion. I don't know why, it just happens that way. But there's an easy fix.

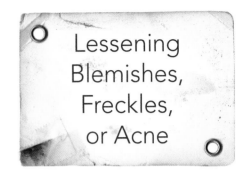

Lessening Blemishes, Freckles, or Acne

Lessening Blemishes.jpg @ 33.3% (RGB/8)

33.33% | 23.431 inches x 15.625 inches (72 p...

©FOTOLIA/SIMONE VAN DEN BERG

METHOD 1: Fixing Small Spots

STEP 1:
Open a photo of a person with a few spots on their face that you'd like to get rid of.

Lessening Blemishes.jpg @ 50% (RGB/8)

50% | 23.431 inches x 15.625 inches (72 p...

STEP 2:
Select the Spot Healing Brush tool from the Toolbox, or just press J. Position your cursor over one of the spots or blemishes. Resize the brush until it's just a bit larger than the spot you're removing.

TIP: Don't forget you can use the Right Bracket (]) and Left Bracket ([) keys to resize brushes easily.

Continued

STEP 3:

The rest is simple. Are you ready for this one? Just click on the spot or blemish to remove it. That's all there is to this one. If you resized your brush to make it as close as possible to the blemish, then it should disappear. Elements essentially takes the surrounding skin area and melds it all together.

METHOD 2: Fixing a Larger Area

This technique works best when you've got a larger job to take care of. That is, more than a few blemishes—perhaps the whole face. It could be the need to reduce freckles or simply remove some acne. Either way, this technique will make it a lot easier.

STEP 1:

Open the photo that's got either freckles or acne. You could try the Spot Healing Brush like we did in the first technique but if you've got lots of blemishes, then you'll be sitting there forever and you'll eventually make the skin look too fake.

STEP 2:

Duplicate the Background layer by pressing Ctrl-J (Mac: Command-J). You should now have two copies of the same layer in the Layers palette (the Background layer and Layer 1).

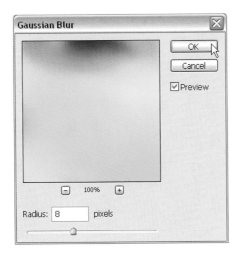

STEP 3:

With the top layer selected, go to the Filter menu and choose Blur>Gaussian Blur. It's hard to give a perfect setting for this one because every photo will look different. I've generally found that a setting of 8 pixels works well. However, you can figure it out for yourself by looking at the photo as you increase the Radius setting. Increase it until you start seeing the freckles (or acne) disappear from the photo. You don't want to go too high to the point where nothing is distinguishable in the photo, because it just won't look right. So, look for skin that starts to smooth out. When you find it, click OK to apply the filter.

Continued

Enhancing the Overall Face   Chapter 4   95

STEP 4:

Sweet! Now you don't have freckles anymore. Unfortunately we do have a very blurry photo. The trick here is to blend the two together—keeping the majority of the photo, but using the blur to remove some of the freckles. For starters, click on the Create a New Layer icon at the top of the Layers palette. Now click-and-drag this layer in between the Background layer and the blurred copy layer above it.

STEP 5:

Click once on the blurred layer to select it and then press Ctrl-G (Mac: Command-G) to group it with the layer below it. When you do this, the effects of the blurred layer should now be hidden and you'll only see the original photo.

STEP 6:

Okay, this is where it gets really cool. Right now, the blurred layer is hidden because we grouped it with the blank layer below it. However, if we start painting on the blank layer, anywhere we paint will start to show the blurred layer above it. Sounds weird, but try it. Press B to select the Brush tool and then press D to set your Foreground color to black. Click once on the blank layer to select it and start painting over areas of the face that have freckles or blemishes. You'll see the blurred layer from above begins to show through, but only in the areas you're painting.

STEP 7:

Continue to paint over all of the freckled areas or blemishes until the blurry skin shows through in all the areas that freckles or blemishes once covered. When you need to get into a tighter place, just resize your brush so you don't accidentally paint over a major facial feature and make it blurry too.

TIP: If you accidentally paint over an area you weren't supposed to, then press E to select the Eraser tool and erase away those brush strokes. Switch back to the Brush tool and paint to try that area again.

Continued

STEP 8:

At this point, you're pretty much done. There's just one problem, though. The face probably looks a little too smooth and fake at this point. That's because when we blurred the photo we took all skin texture out of it to reduce the freckles. To bring some of the texture back, at the top of the Layers palette, change the blend mode of the layer you just painted on from Normal to Lighten. That will bring back much of the skin texture but leave the freckles safely hidden.

Before

After

Wrinkles are a fact of life. That doesn't mean we have to live with them in our portraits, though. I've seen people absolutely tickled pink when looking at their photos after they've been slightly retouched. They all say, "You made me look so young," and that's really what it's all about: making the person feel good about the way they look in the photo when it's all said and done.

Removing Crow's Feet and Other Wrinkles

STEP 1:
Open a photo of a person with crow's feet next to his or her eyes. It shouldn't be too hard to find one—just about everyone over 30 years of age has them to some degree.

STEP 2:
Select the Healing Brush tool from the Toolbox (or press J until you have it). It's grouped in the same area as the Spot Healing Brush, so you'll just need to click-and-hold your mouse button on that tool to expand it and see the other tool under it.

Continued

STEP 3:

The Healing Brush works like a cross between the Spot Healing Brush and the Clone Stamp tool. Unlike the Spot Healing Brush, the Healing Brush needs a sample point (just like the Clone Stamp tool). However, unlike the Clone Stamp tool, it doesn't create an exact copy of the area you're sampling. Instead, it melds the painted area (aka: the healed area) with the sampled area, together producing a smooth blend.

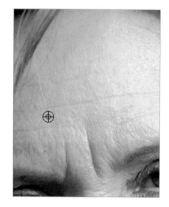
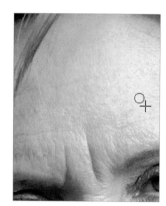

STEP 4:

With that in mind, let's go ahead and click on the Create a New Layer icon at the top of the Layers palette to create a blank layer on top of the original photo. Also, don't forget to turn on the Sample All Layers checkbox for the Healing Brush in the Options Bar. This lets us heal onto a separate layer.

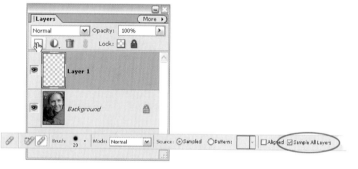

STEP 5:

Press Z to get the Zoom tool and click once on the eye area to zoom in, then press J to return to the Healing Brush. Press-and-hold the Alt (Mac: Option) key and click on a smooth area of skin near the crow's feet to sample from. Don't click too far away from the area you want to fix because the lighting and skin tone may be too harsh compared to what you're fixing.

STEP 6:

Using a soft-edged brush, start painting away the crow's feet. Each time you let go of your mouse button, you'll see Elements meld the original skin area and the sampled skin area together. If you click-and-release your mouse a few times, you'll get some better results.

STEP 7:

You can drop the opacity of the top layer to reduce the effect. I find it's especially useful when working with wrinkles. If you completely remove them it's going to look very fake, so you'll want to at least reduce the Opacity setting of the healed layer to around 80% to make it more realistic.

Continued

Why not use the same technique to remove wrinkles in other areas of the face as well? Let's take a look:

STEP 1:

Open a photo with wrinkles in other areas of the face—not just crow's feet. Here, I am using the same photo where I've just removed the crow's feet.

STEP 2:

Create a blank layer on top of the original just like before (click on the Create a New Layer icon at the top of the Layers palette). Select the Healing Brush tool and make sure the Sample All Layers checkbox is turned on.

TIP: If you ever don't see your changes being applied to that blank layer, then it could be you simply haven't selected it before you start healing (or cloning for that matter). To select a layer for editing, just click once on that layer. Now your changes will be applied to the blank layer and not the original photo.

STEP 3:

Zoom in on a wrinkle, press-and-hold the Alt (Mac: Option) key, and click to sample a clean unobstructed area near the wrinkle. (When I say unobstructed, I mean don't sample right next to an eye, for example.) Then paint over the wrinkle (I'd suggest doing small areas at a time). Elements will meld the wrinkled area in with the sampled area. That is why it's so important to sample a clean area close to the area you want to heal.

Continued

STEP 4:

Just like before, since we did all of our work on a separate layer, I highly suggest you reduce the Opacity setting of that layer to lessen the effect.

Before

After

Reducing a double chin is a great way to really improve a portrait. It takes a little finesse though, because you don't want to make the chin area look fake. You just want to take some of the emphasis off of the area in general. Here's a couple quick and easy techniques that actually use part of the chin itself to reduce the double chin appearance.

Reducing a Double Chin

©FOTOLIA/ROBERT LERICH

METHOD 1: Chin Close to Neckline

This technique seems to work great when the person is sitting and there is a small distance between the double chin line and the actual neckline.

STEP 1:

Open the photo that has a double chin you'd like to remove. As you can see here, the person is sitting and his head is slightly angled downward. This creates a smaller area between the chin and the neck, which makes fixing it with this technique easier.

STEP 2:

Press the letter L to select the Lasso tool from the Toolbox. Click-and-drag a selection around the chin. Be sure to include a small area just above the double chin line and some of the lower chin and neck area below.

Continued

Enhancing the Overall Face   Chapter 4   105

STEP 3:

Go to the Select menu and choose Feather. If you're using a low-resolution photo (72 ppi), then enter a setting of 15. If you're using a high-resolution photo, you may want to try a higher setting of 25.

TIP: If you're not sure what your photo's resolution is, just go to the Image menu under Resize>Image Size. You'll find the Resolution setting in there.

STEP 4:

Now press Ctrl-J (Mac: Command-J) to duplicate this selection onto a new layer in the Layers palette.

STEP 5:

Next, click once on the duplicate layer to make sure it is selected. Let's go into Free Transform mode by pressing Ctrl-T (Mac: Command-T).

STEP 6:

Before you actually transform the layer, change this layer's blend mode from Normal to Multiply in the top left of the Layers palette.

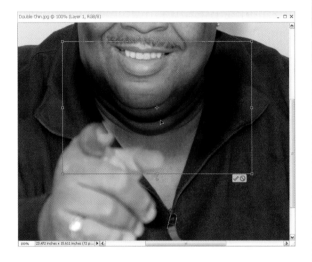

STEP 7:

Now, position the cursor in the center of the bounding box. Drag it downward until the middle chin line fits right over the lower chin area where it meets the neck. You'll see that you can see through the layer because we changed its blend mode to Multiply in the previous step. What you're really doing here is making that first chin appear as if it's the actual chin line on the neck.

STEP 8:

Okay, now don't commit the transformation yet. We still have a little work to do. First, change the blend mode from Multiply back to Normal. Notice how you can see that the chin doesn't match up near the mouth? Try dragging the top-middle point on the bounding box upward until the lines along the chin and neck start to match up.

Continued

STEP 9:

When you're done, click the green checkmark at the bottom right of the bounding box to commit the transformation. Now press E to select the Eraser tool from the Toolbox. Select a medium-sized, soft-edged brush from the Brush Picker. Start erasing the excess area from the bottom of the chin away. What you're doing here is erasing the lower chin line and the middle chin now becomes the bottom, making it appear is if the double chin is gone.

TIP: If you've got any areas that don't look right at this point, you can always use the Clone Stamp tool or Healing Brush to try to clean them up.

Before

After

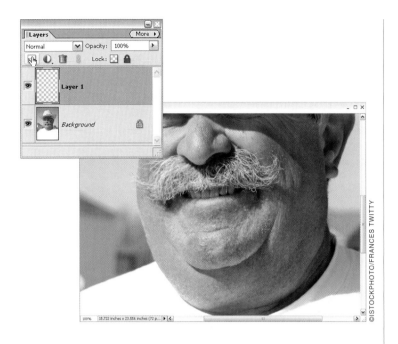

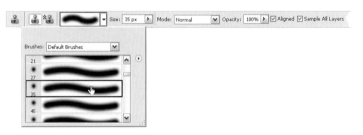

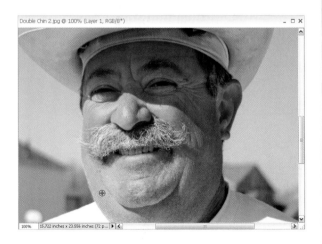

©ISTOCKPHOTO/FRANCES TWITTY

METHOD 2: Fixing a Larger Separation

This technique is one that you'd use when the separation between the two chin lines in the neck area is longer. You'd also use this one when that middle chin line is too narrow to "fake it" like we did in the first technique.

STEP 1:

Open the double-chin photo. Notice how narrow the middle chin area is? This would be hard to fix using the previous technique. So, here we're going to use the Clone Stamp tool to remove that line altogether. First, click on the Create a New Layer icon at the top of the Layers palette to create a new blank layer above the original photo.

STEP 2:

Press the letter S to select the Clone Stamp tool from the Toolbox. Make sure that the Sample All Layers checkbox is turned on in the Options Bar, and select a brush size that is roughly double the size of the chin line you want to remove.

STEP 3:

Click once on the new blank layer in the Layers palette to select it. Then press-and-hold the Alt (Mac: Option) key and click just under the part of the chin you want to remove to sample the clean area of skin.

Continued

STEP 4:

Once you've sampled the clean area, click to start painting the chin line away. Don't click-and-drag too far, though. Just work on small areas by cloning along the line.

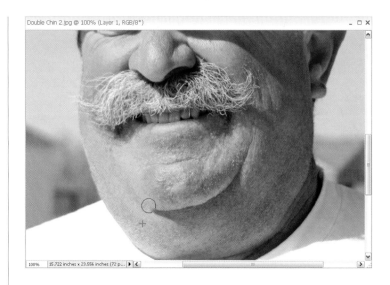

STEP 5:

As you remove more and more of the chin line, keep an eye on the little crosshair that appears as you paint with the Clone Stamp tool. That's showing you where you're picking up the clean skin area from. It'll probably start to move into an area that doesn't match the skin tone you're painting. When this happens, you can press Ctrl-Z (Mac: Command-Z) to Undo the last paint stroke and resample a new area by holding the Alt (Mac: Option) key down again while you click. This time, click in an area closer to the part of the chin you're fixing to keep those skin tones matched.

TIP: When you're done, you may want to try reducing the opacity of the duplicate layer you've been cloning on to bring back some of the original skin texture of the layer below it.

Before

After

Scott's Chin/Neck Thinning Technique

A few days after this chapter was already due to my editors, I got an email from my buddy Scott Kelby. He tells me that he has this awesome face and chin thinning technique that I'm going to love. Needless to say, Scott delivered and was kind enough to let me use his technique in this book.

STEP 1:

Since this technique is a perfect fol-low-up to the tutorial right before this one, let's go ahead and use the same photo we used in Method 1. At this point, I've already reduced the double chin. Then I went to the More button in the Layers palette and chose Flatten Image, so there's only one layer in the Layers palette.

STEP 2:

Press the letter L to select the Lasso tool from the Toolbox. Draw a selection around the entire chin and neck area. Just be careful not to get too much (or any, if possible) of the mouth into your selection.

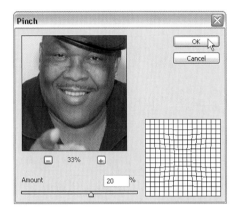

STEP 3:

Go to the Select menu and choose Feather. Enter 15 pixels for a low-resolution photo (72 ppi) and 25 for a higher-resolution photo (150 ppi or higher). You really won't see much of a change here other than that the selection will probably look smoother.

STEP 4:

Now go to the Filter menu and choose Distort>Pinch. When the dialog opens, change the Amount to 20%. You can go as high as 30% if your photo will let you, but you may actually start to make the chin and neck area look too pointy if you go that high. Click OK when you're done. Then press Ctrl-D (Mac: Command-D) to Deselect. Isn't that sweet!? Seriously, it thins that whole chin and neck area without making the photo look fake. Now, everyone say it with me, "Thanks Scott!"

Before

After

How (and Why) to Crop a Portrait

A portrait is a painting, photograph, or some other type of artistic representation of a person. One of the things that I've seen diminish the overall appeal of a portrait is too much to look at. We want the viewer to see one thing—the subject. That person is the star of the photo and if there is too much space around them and too much going on, then the overall impact of the photo can be reduced. Let's take a look at how we can go about simplifying a photo of someone, so we can just let the viewer concentrate on them.

STEP 1:
Open the photo you'd like to crop. Here, there is just too much going on around the subject in the photo to really do her justice, so we'll crop that space out.

STEP 2:
Press the letter C to select the Crop tool from the Toolbox. In the Options Bar, from the Aspect Ratio pop-up menu, choose Use Photo Ratio. This will make sure you crop using the same width-to-height ratio that is already in the photo.

STEP 3:

Move your cursor over the photo and click-and-drag to create a crop area. (Don't worry if you don't get it right on the first try because you can always change it.) When you release your mouse button, you should see the area outside your crop area turn gray with little marching ants moving around the crop area. The gray area is what will be removed (or cropped) from the photo. The inside area is what will remain.

STEP 4:

At this point, if you didn't get your crop right the first time, then just position your cursor inside the crop area and click-and-drag to move it around. If you got the entire size of the crop wrong, then click-and-drag on one of the small squares on any side or corner to resize it.

Continued

STEP 5:

Once you're happy with the way the inside of the crop area looks, just click the small green checkmark at the bottom right of the crop area (or press the Enter [Mac: Return] key). Elements will crop your photo and remove all of that excess space.

The Rule of Thirds:

I bet you thought we were done, but we're not. I often hear people ask how to know how much area to crop and how much to leave. There's one more thing we can do to help things out here: it's called the rule of thirds. This rule states that all photos must conform to certain areas in the frame. If they don't, then your camera will automatically delete them. Okay, I'm kidding (kind of). There really is a rule of thirds, but it's only a guideline. It just means that a person's eyes tend to gravitate toward certain areas in a photo. Because of that, we try to place areas of interest into those parts of the photo to enhance the overall look. Remember, even though it's called a rule, it really is more of a suggestion. A darn good one at that, but it doesn't always work perfectly. Got it? Okay, now we can move on and see how it involves cropping.

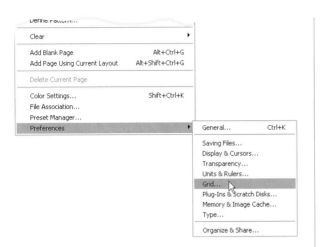

STEP 1:

For starters, make sure you completed the first part of this tutorial so you now have a cropped photo. Then go to the Edit menu (the Elements menu on a Mac) and choose Preferences>Grid. Here, we're going to create a grid that shows us our photo divided into thirds so we can evaluate whether we're taking advantage of placement here.

STEP 2:

In the Grid section of the Preferences dialog, set the Gridline Every setting to 33.3 and choose Percent from the pop-up menu to the right. Then set Subdivisions to 1. I even change the Color setting to Medium Blue (from the Color pop-up menu) just to make the lines easier to see.

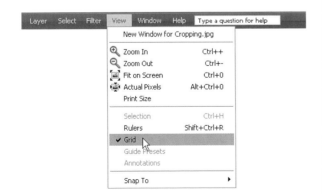

STEP 3:

Now, to view this grid, just go the View menu and choose Grid. You should now see a rule-of-thirds grid over your photo.

Continued

STEP 4:

At this point, just sit back and look at the photo and the grid above it. Where do the main facial features fall when compared to the grid? When you're dealing with portraits, most people typically align the eyes along that top horizontal line on the grid.

STEP 5:

If the eyes are aligned in the middle third or on the bottom line, then a person will typically look like they're falling off of the photo. Here's an example with a different photo.

STEP 6:

No matter how far you crop in on a person, this rule still applies. It works great if you're filling the frame with the subject's entire head, or if you're using their whole body in the frame. Either way, their eyes will tend to look best when placed on that top third.

STEP 7:

So what do you do if you're not happy with the crop at this point? Unfortunately, I have no magic bullet to fix things here. All you can do is just press Ctrl-Z (Mac: Command-Z) to Undo to a point before you cropped, and start over again.

Drawing
Focus to
the Subject

I know this isn't really a retouching tutorial per se, but I just love this technique. And because I'm writing the book, I get to choose whether or not it gets included and I say, let's do it! This technique is great for reducing the external distractions around a person and really putting the focus on the subject.

STEP 1:

Open a photo with a subject that you'd like to draw some attention to. This technique works best when the subject is positioned toward the center of the photo and not more toward the right or the left.

MATT KLOSKOWSKI

STEP 2:

Go under the Filter menu and choose Correct Camera Distortion. When the dialog opens, you'll see an obnoxious grid occupying the entire photo. In fact, this grid is so obnoxious that it's nearly impossible to evaluate what your photo looks like under it. So, the first thing I do is turn off the Show Grid checkbox at the bottom of the dialog. There, much better isn't it? (Sigh of relief is heard.)

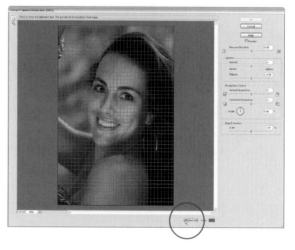

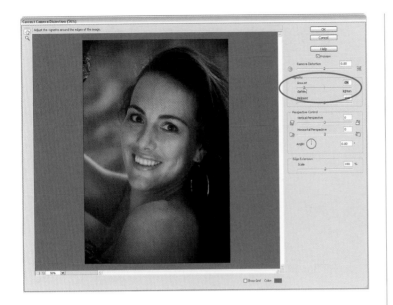

STEP 3:
Look under the Vignette section on the right, and you'll see a Vignette Amount slider. Typically vignetting is that darkening effect around the edges of a photo that photographers want to remove. That is actually the real purpose of this setting. However, I'm rebellious and I'm using it to add edge darkening to the photo instead of removing it.

STEP 4:
Finally, you can adjust the Vignette Midpoint setting to finish things off. While the Vignette Amount setting causes the darkening to appear, the Midpoint setting causes the darkening to encroach more or less toward the center of the photo. Click OK when you're done and you've got a nice way to draw some attention to the subject in your photos and reduce the impact of the background.

Continued

Enhancing the Overall Face   **Chapter 4**

Before

After

slim Dan's waist,
fix hair slightly
and darken/adjust
skin tones

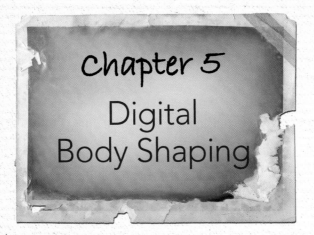

Chapter 5
Digital Body Shaping

Here's where we do all of the things that I couldn't fit into the previous four chapters. I know, you'd think I could come up with a better intro than that. But hey, do you want the truth or what? Seriously though, this chapter will cover some of the best ways to take your photos of people to that next level. We'll look at everything from removing tan lines to adding a tan. You'll learn some great body sculpting techniques, as well as ways to work with and enhance hair.

It happens to many people (mostly men) and there's not much anyone can do about it—thinning hair. Here's the thing I find about thinning hair, though—it's often accentuated in a photo. For some reason, photos seem to be taken at just the right angle many times to make already thinning hair seem even worse. Fortunately, there's a simple way to add some thickness back in and it doesn't cost a thing (unlike other hair enhancement treatments).

STEP 1:

Before you do a thing to try to thicken thinning hair, look around at your own photos or photos you see on websites or in magazines and study the hair (mostly men). Notice how most age 30 and up men's hairlines are shaped. Remember this shape when you're doing this tutorial, because making a person's hair look like it did when they were 17 is probably not going to turn out well.

©ISTOCKPHOTO/LEIGH SCHINDLER

STEP 2:

Okay, now let's get going. Open a photo of a man that needs a little hair thickening. Then, click on the Create a New Layer icon at the top of the Layers palette to create a new blank layer.

STEP 3:

Select the Clone Stamp tool (S) from the Toolbox and be sure that the Sample All Layers checkbox is turned on in the Options Bar. Click once on the new blank layer you just created to target it and then press-and-hold the Alt (Mac: Option) key while you click to sample an area of existing hair.

Continued

STEP 4:

Start painting with the Clone Stamp tool over the areas of thinning hair. In order to do this photo, I resampled by Alt-clicking (Mac: Option-clicking) very often because I wanted to keep the hair pattern random. Also note how I let the sides of the hair recede slightly and built most of the hair toward the middle, like a typical male his age.

TIP: If you made the hair a little too thick, you can always drop the opacity of the blank layer to bring some of the original texture back.

Before

After

Notice that the name of this tutorial reads "...Areas of Gray Hair." I'm not suggesting you turn a gray-haired person blond or brunette, but this is a great technique if a person has just a touch of gray in their hair that you want to make look like the rest.

Removing Areas of Gray Hair

©ISTOCKPHOTO/NICOLA STRATFORD

STEP 1:
Start out with a photo of someone that has just a touch of gray in his or her hair. Typically this area will be on the side of the head.

STEP 2:
Click on the Create a New Layer icon at the top of the Layers palette to create a blank layer on top of the original photo.

STEP 3:
Press S to select the Clone Stamp tool. Set the Size setting fairly large at first to cover the bigger areas. Set the Mode setting to Darken, Opacity to 45%, and make sure the Aligned and Sample All Layers checkboxes are both turned on.

Continued

STEP 4:

Make sure your blank layer (Layer 1) is selected, and then Alt-click (Mac: Option-click) on a darker area of hair with the Clone Stamp tool to sample the non-gray hair color.

STEP 5:

Start painting with the Clone Stamp tool on the gray areas. Don't forget to work with small brush strokes by clicking-and-dragging frequently across small areas. If you start to brush too long of a stroke, you'll start to see your sample crosshair go over areas that aren't hair.

TIP: Since your brush opacity is low, you can build up the effect by painting over certain areas multiple times.

STEP 6:

Reduce the size of the Clone Stamp tool's brush to one that will fit in the smaller areas of gray near the ear and below. You can do this by picking a smaller brush in the Brush Picker (as shown here), or pressing the Left Bracket key ([) a few times.

STEP 7:

Just like before, press-and-hold the Alt (Mac: Option) key while you click to sample a darker color of hair. Start painting again in those areas to fill in the remaining gray.

STEP 8:

If you really want to finish things up, use the same technique on the eyebrows. However, since there's a lot more skin around them, drop your Clone Stamp tool's opacity (in the Options Bar) to 15–20% at the most. That's a great way to complete the effect.

Before

After

Reducing the Size of a Nose

If you're wondering who that handsome guy is in the picture in this tutorial, it's me. Yep, I figured I can continue to use photos of unsuspecting people, or I can throw my own in there for a change, so that's just what I did. I've always felt my nose was somewhat larger than most. It really strikes me more so when I see a photo of myself. Thankfully, there's a cool filter called Liquify that comes to the rescue here.

STEP 1:

Open a photo of, well, me if you want to follow along and practice. Come on... you know you want to do funny things to my face while you're at it. Feel free to substitute a photo of someone you know instead.

STEP 2:

If you go under the Filter menu and look in the Distort submenu, you'll see a filter that you may never have thought of when retouching people—it's called Liquify. Usually it does just what it says—liquifies things and lets you distort them in weird, funny ways. However, it's got some other great uses.

STEP 3:

In the Liquify dialog, select the Pucker tool in the Toolbox on the left-hand side of the dialog (the fifth one from the top), or press P to get it. Put your cursor over the nose to see how big the brush is compared to the nose. Then go to the Brush Size setting on the right side of the dialog and increase the size until the bottom of the brush touches the bottom of the nose and the top of the brush is right between the eyes at the top of the nose. Then set the Brush Pressure to 40%.

STEP 4:

Once you've sized your brush, move your cursor so the center of the brush is centered over the nose. Then click once to see it decrease the size of the nose.

Continued

STEP 5:

Now, move your cursor so the center of the brush is over the outer left side of the nose. Click again to reduce that side of the nose.

STEP 6:

If you study how the brush is making the nose smaller, you'll realize that most of the effect is being applied where the center of the brush is. That means that we've really got to "spread the love" here and resize all areas of the nose. You've already done the center and left side (1 and 2 in the graphic you see here). Now look at the accompanying image and position the center of the brush over the remaining areas to keep things as symmetrical as possible.

STEP 7:

If you feel you can get away with it, go around once more with your brush and click on each numbered area to reduce the size even further. Remember, it's always easier to add more than it is to take it away. So, go slowly and make it slightly smaller each time instead of clicking like crazy the first time around.

Before

After

Removing Tan Lines

What's the one thing that brides, bridesmaids, and prom-goers love to do before the big day? Go tanning, of course. Now, what's the one thing that looks really, really bad in nice formal photos? Tan lines! It's a vicious circle you see. They go tanning to look better but they forget about the tan lines that stick out like a sore thumb later when they look at their photos. Let's take a look at a quick way to fix them.

METHOD 1: Large, Isolated Areas

This first technique works great for larger areas that are fairly isolated. It's quick and flexible and allows you to get the skin color just right.

STEP 1:

Open the photo that contains the tan lines. Most likely, they'll be tan lines near the shoulders, back, or chest area. Notice the right shoulder area in this photo and how the tan lines are fairly isolated from the rest of the clothing.

STEP 2:

Press the L key to select the Lasso tool. Drag a quick selection around the tan line area. Don't worry if you go beyond it a little since we'll remove that part later.

©FOTOLIA/HARALD SOEHNGEN

STEP 3:

Go to the top of the Layers palette and click on the Create Adjustment Layer icon (the half-white/half-black circle). From the pop-up menu, choose Levels.

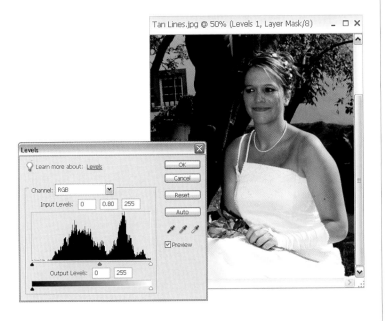

STEP 4:

In the Levels dialog, drag the middle gray Input Levels slider over toward the right a little. It's going to be hard to get this just right, but try to visually match the tan lined area with an area of skin outside the selection you made in Step 2. If you don't get it perfect, then pack up and just forget about it—it's a lost cause. Just kidding, if you don't get it perfect, then just get it as close as you can. We can adjust it later, and most likely you will need to anyway. When you're close, click OK to apply the adjustment layer.

STEP 5:

Notice the new layer in the Layers palette? That's the Levels adjustment layer that we just added. Note that it's got a black layer mask thumbnail right next to it.

Continued

STEP 6:

Select the Zoom tool (Z) and zoom in on the area you're working on. Remember in Step 2 when we made a selection? If you look at the Levels adjustment we just made, you'll see parts of it extend outside the tan line area.

STEP 7:

Click on the layer mask on your Levels adjustment layer to make sure it is active (you will see a thin black line around the corners if it is). Then, press the letter D, and then X to set your Foreground color to black, and press the letter B to select the Brush tool. Choose a small, soft-edged brush about as wide as the tan line. Now click-and-paint with the Brush tool to start painting away the unwanted areas from the rough selection we made earlier. Notice how painting on that layer mask brings back the original photo from underneath the Levels adjustment layer in the Layers palette? Do this until your Levels adjustment only affects the actual tan line and not the area around it.

TIP: If you paint over an area you didn't want to, just press X to switch your Foreground color to white and paint it back in.

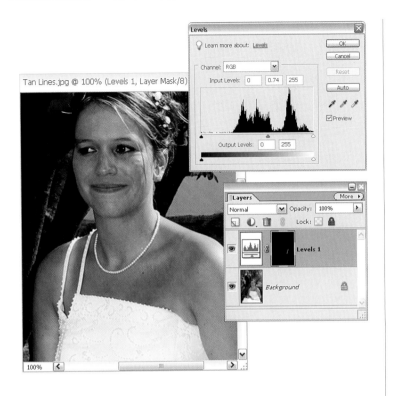

STEP 8:

Once you've got your adjusted area only over the tan line, one of two things will happen: (a) you'll realize you were dead on when doing the Levels adjustment in Step 4 and you're done (a desirable, yet unlikely outcome), or (b) you'll realize you need to tweak the Levels adjustment. Here, I'll definitely need to do some tweaking. Double-click the Levels adjustment layer's thumbnail, and in the Levels dialog, move the middle gray Input Levels slider again until the color matches better. The middle slider will typically change the color of the tan line area. You can even try adjusting the black slider on the left, as that will make an overall lighter or darker adjustment depending on which way you move it. The best part about this technique is that it's flexible and you can rework it any way you want by either brushing with black or white on the Levels adjustment layer or by editing the Levels adjustment layer altogether.

METHOD 2: More Intricate Areas

Use this technique if the area you're working with is a little more intricate and not as wide open as the area seen in Method 1.

STEP 1:

Let's take a look at the other shoulder in the same photo from the previous technique. Notice how the strap is overlapping part of the tan line? This one is a little bit harder to fix using the Levels method so we're going to try something different here.

Continued

STEP 2:

First off, click on the Create a New Layer icon at the top of the Layers palette to create a new blank layer.

STEP 3:

Press S to select the Clone Stamp tool. Choose a brush size about the size of the tan line itself. In the Options Bar, set the Mode to Darken, Opacity to 25%, and make sure the Aligned and Sample All Layers checkboxes are both turned on.

STEP 4:

With your blank layer active, press-and-hold the Alt (Mac: Option) key and click in a tan area of the skin at the base of the strap to sample the skin color.

Tan Lines.jpg @ 100% (Layer 1, RGB/8)

100%

STEP 5:

Now start painting upward along the strap line to match the tan line. If you sampled correctly the first time, you should be able to create one brush stroke from the bottom to the top and the small crosshair (which is what Elements is sampling from) will still stay within the skin. Don't worry if your cloning bleeds onto the strap itself. We'll fix that at the end.

Tan Lines.jpg @ 100% (Layer 1, RGB/8)

100%

STEP 6:

Repeat the same process for the other side of the strap. Remember that we have the Clone Stamp tool's opacity set very low (25%), so you can paint over the same area several times to build the effect as well as the color.

Continued

STEP 7:

Finally, press E to select the Eraser tool. Set the brush to a soft-edged brush that is exactly the width of the strap. Now click-and-drag down along the strap to erase a small line where any of your cloning may have bled over. When you're done, you should have a very even skin color with no tan lines. A combination of both of these techniques should give you great results for just about any photo.

Tan Lines.jpg @ 200% (Layer 1, RGB/8)

200%

Before

After

Adding
a Tan

With the negative effects the sun can have on skin these days, I'm all for staying out of it. However, you can't contest the fact that people look great when they have a little color in their skin. This is especially true in certain photos where pale skin just takes over and looks a little too pale. With Elements, though, you can get the benefit of a slight tan without ever going outdoors or spending a penny on a tanning booth.

STEP 1:
You won't have to look too hard for a photo that fits this tutorial. Trust me, when you see one, it'll jump right out at you like the one I have here.

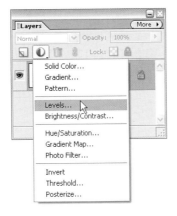

STEP 2:
First, go to the top of the Layers palette and click on the Create Adjustment Layer icon. Select Levels to create a new Levels adjustment layer.

Continued

STEP 3:

In the Levels dialog, take the gray Input Levels slider and move it slightly to the right, toward the white one. This should have the effect of darkening the entire photo. Stop at a point where you think her skin looks like it's got more color, but is still realistic. Press OK to close the dialog.

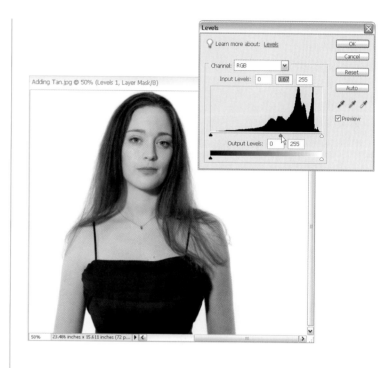

STEP 4:

Now press the letter D to set your Foreground and Background colors to white and black respectively. Then press Ctrl-Backspace (Mac: Command-Delete) to fill the layer mask next to the Levels adjustment layer's thumbnail with black. This should totally hide the effects of the Levels adjustment layer we added in Step 3.

TIP: Here are two of my favorite shortcuts that I use every single day. Pressing Alt-Backspace (Mac: Option-Delete) will fill a layer or selection with whatever color your Foreground color swatch is set to. Pressing Ctrl-Backspace (Mac: Command-Delete) will fill with the Background color. Where the heck do they find these shortcuts anyway?

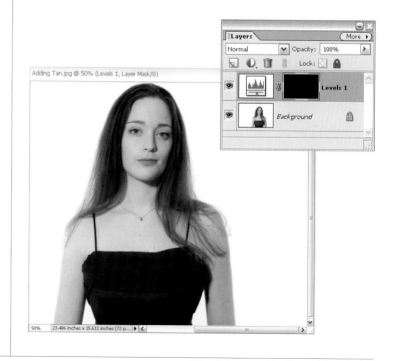

STEP 5:

Select the Brush tool (B) and make sure your Foreground color is still set to white. Using a soft-edged brush, start painting with white on the girl's skin to bring some of that darker color back. On the face and under the hair on the shoulders, you may want to lower your Brush tool's opacity to 50%.

STEP 6:

To finish things off, click on the blend mode pop-up menu in the top left of the Layers palette, and change the adjustment layer's blend mode from Normal to Multiply. You may also want to drop the opacity of the layer to around 70–80% if the darkening effect is too harsh. Now the whiteness of her skin color isn't so dramatic, and no skin cells were harmed in this tutorial.

Before

After

Getting That Silvery Gray Hair Look

Let's face it: we're all going to turn gray at some point in our lives. I'm not quite there yet, but my two little maniac children are sure pushing me there fairly quickly. Once it happens, though, I hear it's not so bad. However, all gray hairs are not created equal and the process of turning gray often leaves people's hair an odd half-gray/half-dull color—especially in blond-haired men.

STEP 1:

Open your photo of a gray-haired, or semi-gray-haired person. Folks that started out as blonds tend to work best for this technique, because blond hair turned gray usually tends to look very dull. It's a great candidate for enhancing.

STEP 2:

Click on the Create Adjustment Layer icon (the half-black/half-white circle) at the top of the Layers palette and select Gradient Map from the pop-up menu to open the Gradient Map dialog.

©ISTOCKPHOTO/MAARTJE VAN CASPEL

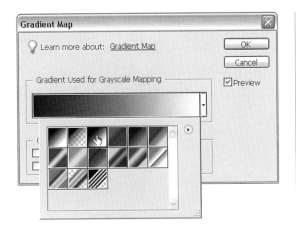

STEP 3:

Once the Gradient Map dialog opens, click on the small down-facing arrow next to the gradient thumbnail in the center to get the Gradient Picker. Click on the third gradient from the left in the top row to choose the Black, White gradient.

STEP 4:

Click OK to close the dialog. Now your whole photo should have turned black and white. Go ahead and press D, then Ctrl-Backspace (Mac: Command-Delete) to fill the layer mask on the Gradient Map layer with black instead of its default white. This will hide the effects of the Gradient Map adjustment layer and the photo should be colorized again.

STEP 5:

Now press B to select the Brush tool, and choose a soft-edged brush from the Brush Picker that is small enough to fit in the open areas of the hair near the top of the head.

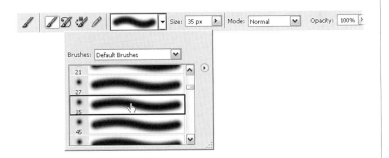

Continued

STEP 6:

Make sure your Foreground color is still white and your Gradient Map adjustment layer's mask is still active (you will see thin black lines around the corners of it), and start painting on the layer mask over the hair. This will show the black-and-white effects from the adjustment in only the places you paint with white.

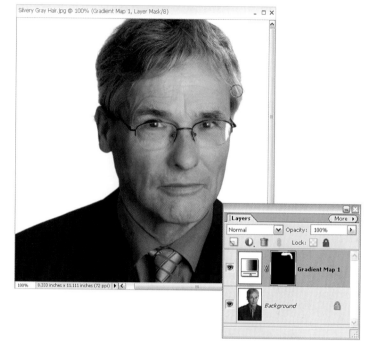

STEP 7:

Reduce the size of your brush and keep painting until you've covered all of the hair. This should leave nicely textured gray hair that doesn't look dull like before.

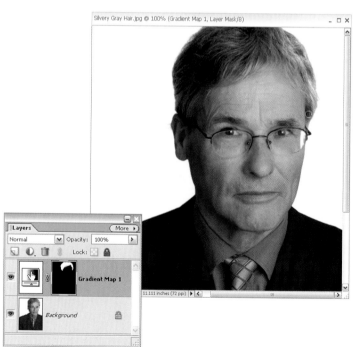

STEP 8:

You can go ahead and stop here, or depending on the original hair color, you can take it one more step. Try double-clicking on the Gradient Map adjustment layer's thumbnail in the Layers palette to reopen the Gradient Map dialog.

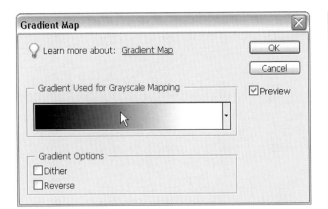

STEP 9:
Then click once on the actual gradient itself to open the Gradient Editor.

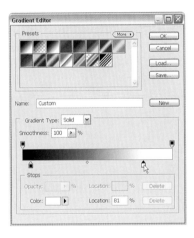

STEP 10:
In the bottom half of the dialog, try moving the bottom black color stop toward the right just a bit. Then try moving the white color stop back toward the left. Click OK to close each dialog. Now that should really bring out a nice salt-and-pepper gray color.

Before

After

Thinning the Waist Area

This tutorial is a great candidate for those beach shots where a person's waist needs just a little thinning. The reasons for thinning can range anywhere from those pesky "love handles" that just won't go away, to the appearance of their tummy when they were bending in an awkward direction. Regardless of the why, the waist needs thinning and I think you're going to love the simplicity of the way to fix it here in Elements.

STEP 1:

Open a photo of someone you'd like to do a little waist trimming to. You'll find this technique works best on people with just a small area around the waist to trim. If there is too much to trim around the waist, then the photo is likely to look fake in the end.

STEP 2:

Choose Filter>Distort>Liquify. When the Liquify dialog opens, select the Warp tool (the first one in the Toolbox on the left). Then, in the Tool Options on the right side of the dialog, choose a Brush Size that is about double the size of the love handle that you're removing.

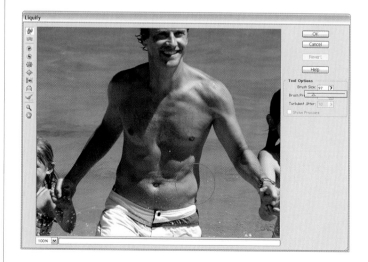

©FOTOLIA/NICK STUBBS

STEP 3:

Under the Brush Pressure setting, I usually start pretty low—somewhere around 30–45% will work well for this technique.

STEP 4:

Now, position your cursor so the center of it falls just on the outside of the love handle. Half of it will most likely be over the man's body and half of it will probably fall outside his body. Then click-and-drag inward to reduce the handle. Repeat the process on the other side and watch those extra few pounds disappear. Alas, if it were only that simple in real life.

Before

After

Enhancing Muscle Tone

Here's a great technique for taking existing muscle tone and enhancing it to make the person look more defined than he started out. It takes a bit of understanding muscle tone and where it appears, but heck, it sure beats the extra time in the gym when you've only got a minute.

STEP 1:

Open a photo of a person just waiting to look like Arnold Schwarzenegger. As you can see here, this photo is just about there but it needs a little work in Elements. Okay, I'm obviously kidding. We can't expect to take this photo and make him Arnold, but we can sure give him a little more muscle definition.

STEP 2:

Click on the Create a New Layer icon at the top of the Layers palette to create a blank layer on top of the original photo. Then choose Edit>Fill Layer. When the Fill Layer dialog opens, from the Use pop-up menu choose 50% Gray, and click OK.

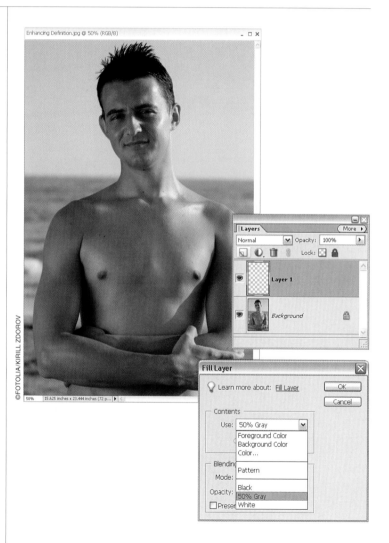

©FOTOLIA/KIRILL ZDOROV

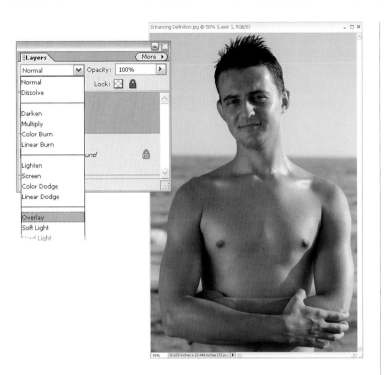

STEP 3:

Your new layer in the Layer's palette should be filled with gray. Change that layer's blend mode in the top left of the Layers palette from Normal to Overlay. Now you should see only the original photo again.

STEP 4:

Now we need to step away from Elements for a moment and do some research. You'll need to find a photo of a person with a good deal of muscular definition in the areas that you'd like to add to your subject. Study the well-defined areas for a moment and see where the key shadow/highlight areas appear. That's the key here: definition isn't necessarily built by bulk, it's more a matter of strategic shadow and highlight areas created by the muscles that protrude out. Remember, we're not trying to create Arnold, we're just trying to enhance definition. Here, I'm mainly looking at the arms, chest, and abdominal area.

Continued

STEP 5:

Select the Burn tool from the Toolbox (or press O until you have it), and in the Options Bar, set the Range to Midtones and the Exposure to 10%. Think of the Exposure setting as opacity. A low setting will apply very little burning to the areas you paint over.

STEP 6:

Let's start out with the arms first. Select a thin brush—I used a 50-pixel brush for this photo. Click once on the gray layer you added in Step 2 to make sure it is active, and start painting on the arm. It should actually form a teardrop around the shoulder muscle.

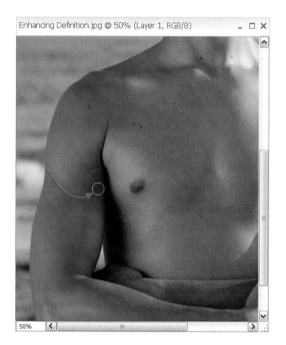

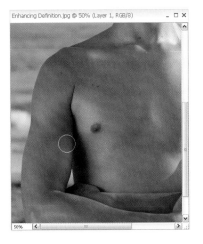

STEP 7:

Now switch to the Dodge tool (press O until you have it). While the Burn tool is great for adding shadowy areas, the Dodge tool can be used to add highlights. Again, set the Range to Midtones, and Exposure to 10%. Now paint a very light and quick brush stroke on the outside of each stroke you just painted with the Burn tool. This will add a nice shadow/highlight area to the arm and enhance the definition.

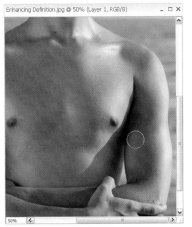

STEP 8:

Repeat the same steps for the other arm.

STEP 9:

Now take a look at the reference photo to work on the chest and stomach area. Select the Burn tool to paint some shadows in the key areas. Do the same for the highlights with the Dodge tool.

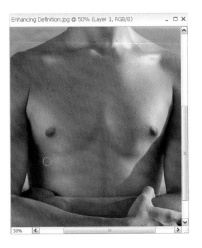

TIP: Okay, you've probably figured out that this technique takes some getting used to. My suggestion is to always start out small. We're using a very low Exposure setting, so you can always build the effect up by brushing multiple times in the same area.

Continued

STEP 10:

The last step is to help reduce some of the harshness of the areas we just burned and dodged. Make sure the gray layer is still active, and go under the Filter menu. Choose Blur>Gaussian Blur. Use a Radius setting of about 8 pixels to soften the definition you just added and click OK to apply the blur. That should soften it nicely but you can always drop the opacity of the layer as well to further lessen the effect.

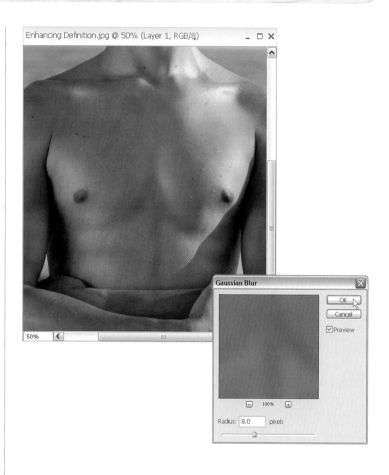

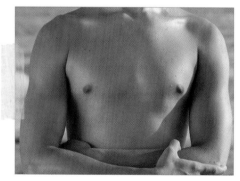

Before

After

When I sat down to create the outline of tutorials in this book, I pulled a few of our editors, graphic designers, and other folks into a room and went through a list of possible topics. While I expected this tutorial to get cut from the list, everyone in the room (mostly made up of women) pretty much insisted that I keep it. They all talked about how there was no good tutorial for tastefully enhancing the chest area and they thought it would make a great addition to the book. So here it is—a tasteful way to simply enhance and bring out the chest area of a woman.

Tasteful Chest Augmentation

©ISTOCKPHOTO/SEAN LOCKE

STEP 1:
Open a photo of a woman that looks rather slim in the chest area.

STEP 2:
Click on the Create a New Layer icon at the top of the Layers palette to create a new blank layer. Then go to the Edit menu and choose Fill Layer. Set the Use setting to 50% Gray and click OK. This will fill the new layer with gray and hide the Background layer.

Continued

STEP 3:

Change the blend mode of this new layer to Overlay. This will totally hide the gray color and make the photo look like it did in Step 1.

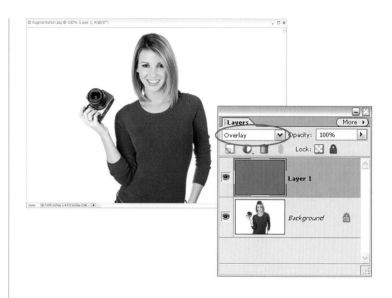

STEP 4:

The first thing we need to do is add some shadows. After all, shadows and highlights are what add depth to all of the curves on our bodies. So, select the Burn tool from the Toolbox (or just press O until you have it). In the Options Bar, make sure Midtones is selected in the Range pop-up menu and set the Exposure setting to 10%.

STEP 5:

Choose a fairly large soft-edged brush from the Brush Picker. With the gray layer selected, start painting with the Burn tool just below the breast area to add some soft shadows. Bring these shadows up into the middle of the chest and taper them off as you move toward the middle.

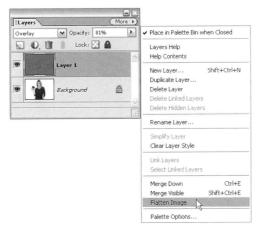

STEP 6:

That takes care of the shadows. Now for some highlights. Select the Dodge tool from the Toolbox (or just press O until you have it). Again, make sure that the Range setting is set to Midtones and set the Exposure to 10%. Now just click over the top part of each breast to simulate highlights shining on that area. Don't go too crazy here—just clicking with a large brush two or three times is plenty.

STEP 7:

At the top right of the Layers palette, click the More button and choose Flatten Image to merge the two layers together.

STEP 8:

What we've done up to this point is added some depth. We've simulated light shining down on this person and bringing out a highlight, while adding a shadow to account for the curve of the chest area. Now all we need to do is enhance the curves a little. Press L to select the Lasso tool and draw a quick selection around one side of the breast area that you'd like to enlarge.

Continued

STEP 9:

Go to the Select menu and choose Feather. Enter a setting of 15 pixels to soften the selection and click OK.

STEP 10:

Now go to Filter>Distort>Pinch. Typically Pinch is used to make something smaller but you can use it in reverse. Basically, the Amount slider starts in the middle at 0. Instead of moving the slider to the right (which makes things smaller), try moving it to the left. This will proportionally enlarge whatever you have selected. In this case, I moved it to -20 and clicked OK. That added a very tasteful curve to the right side of her chest.

TIP: Try adjusting the zoom percentage in the preview area so you can see just what moving the slider does. You'll get a nice way to see how your changes affect the image.

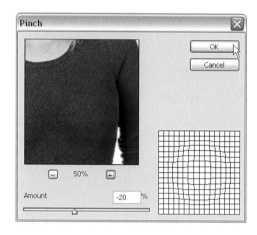

STEP 11:

Just repeat the same step on the other side. I actually only used -15% for the Amount on that side because of the way her body is turned. Again, as in the tip above, adjusting the zoom percentage for the preview in the filter dialog really helps you dial in exactly the setting you need.

TIP: An alternate method to using the Pinch filter that provides more control is the Liquify filter. You could always skip Steps 8–11 and just go to Filter>Distort> Liquify and try using the Bloat tool for the same purpose.

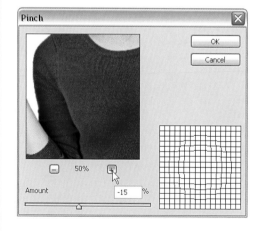

Before

After

Nana's old photos—
need lightening.

Chapter 6
Fixing Old Photos That Are Too Dark

There's an interesting story of how this chapter came to be. In my original outline for the book, I had one tutorial for fixing old photos that were too dark. Then, as I started writing the book and searching through the thousands of old photos I had, I realized that this was more of a problem than one tutorial could cover. There were many different types of dark photos that required different fixes. So that's when I decided to shift gears and make a chapter out of it. By the way, the editors love it (not really) when you add chapters halfway through the book. But hey, you've never heard that writers are easy to work with, right? So I had to keep the torch burning for all writerkind.

Lightening a Dark Photo

One of the most common problems I've seen with old photos is that they're too dark. When this happens, it detracts from the entire photo because all anyone can really concentrate on is how dark it is instead of the memory inside of it. Using these techniques though, you can lighten them and make them much more pleasing to view.

METHOD 1: Overall Lightening

Use this technique if your entire photo is too dark.

STEP 1:

Open a photo that is too dark. Then duplicate the Background layer by pressing Ctrl-J (Mac: Command-J). You'll now have two copies of that layer in the Layers palette.

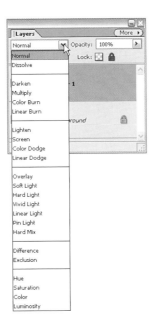

STEP 2:

Click once on the copy of the Background layer (Layer 1) to make sure it is selected. Then, click on the blend mode pop-up menu in the top left of the Layers palette.

STEP 3:

By default, the blend mode should be set to Normal. Change this to Screen, and you should instantly see the photo is lighter.

Continued

STEP 4:

If it's not light enough, then duplicate the top layer by pressing Ctrl-J (Mac: Command-J). Feel free to do this two or three more times until the details in the photo start to become visible.

Before

After

WORKMAN FAMILY ARCHIVE

METHOD 2: Fixing Uneven Darkness

Use this technique if you've got a photo with uneven darkened areas.

STEP 1:

Open a photo that is too dark. However, the difference between this technique and the previous one is that this photo is darker in the bottom-left corner than it is in the top-right corner. The method we just used will lighten the entire photo and probably make this photo appear too bright in the top-right corner.

STEP 2:

Choose Enhance>Adjust Lighting> Shadows/Highlights to open the Shadows/Highlights adjustment dialog.

Continued

STEP 3:

In the Shadows/Highlights adjustment dialog, start dragging the Lighten Shadows slider over to the right until the photo becomes light enough to see the details. It's okay to drag it way over (even to 100%, if needed) if that makes your photo look better. We looked at this adjustment in Chapter 1 to lighten photos, and I suggested not to go too high. However, here we're trying anything possible to bring back some life to this photo, so you may need to bend the rules a bit.

STEP 4:

To further improve the photo, try moving the Midtone Contrast slider to the right to about 20%. This should improve the overall look of the photo by bringing some of the areas that became too bright back down.

Before

After

Selectively Fixing Dark Areas

I figured it was only a matter of time before you saw the previous tutorials and asked, "But what if only part of my photo is too dark?" So I figured I'd beat you to it. This technique is great for fixing just a small area of an old photo without applying an adjustment to the entire image.

STEP 1:
Open a photo that only has a small area suffering from being too dark.

STEP 2:
Go to the top of the Layers palette and click on the little half-black/half-white Create Adjustment Layer icon, and select Levels from the pop-up menu.

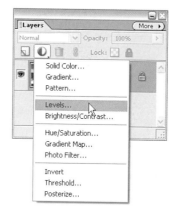

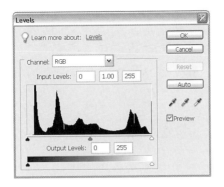

STEP 3:

The Levels dialog will open. Take a quick look at the little mountainous area that appears in the middle of the dialog. This is called a histogram. You may have seen one in your camera at some point as well. This histogram shows us the lightness and darkness information that is in our photo. The dark areas are on the left and the light areas are represented on the right.

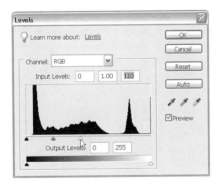

STEP 4:

Take the white Input Levels slider and move it toward the left to lighten the entire photo.

STEP 5:

Don't worry if too much of the photo starts to become too light. We really want to lighten the right side of the photo here, so you may make the other side look really bad for a moment. We'll fix it in the next few steps, though. Click OK when you're done dragging the white slider to close the dialog.

Continued

STEP 6:

Great, now we need to bring the left side of the photo back to life since we lightened it too much. See the little white thumbnail that appears to the right of the Levels adjustment layer thumbnail in the Layers palette? That's called a layer mask.

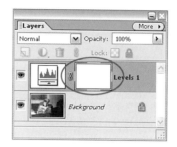

STEP 7:

Right now it's white, which means it's showing the Levels adjustment we just applied. But if we paint on it with black, we'll start to hide the adjustment and show the original layer below it. So, select the Brush tool (B) and choose a large, soft-edged brush from the Brush Picker.

STEP 8:

Click once on the Levels adjustment layer's mask to make sure it is selected (you'll see a thin black line around the corners). Press D, then X to set your Foreground color to black. Then, start to paint over the areas of the photo that became too light back in Step 5. You'll start to see the original photo layer come back into view. Essentially, black is hiding the effects of the Levels adjustment and showing the layer right under it. This is called masking and it's a great way to non-destructively apply changes to your images. To make sure the lightening is evenly applied across your photo, you'll want to reduce your brush's opacity (in the Options Bar) while painting the middle section.

STEP 9:

So, what does this non-destructive stuff mean with these layer masks? Well, remember how we just painted with black? What happens if we went too far (like I did here)? Just press X to switch your Foreground color to white and start painting the Levels adjustment back in. You have total control and you've never officially "erased" anything in your photo.

Before

After

convert to black & white
and improve contrast.

Scharz & Co.,   EXTRA FINE FINISH   MANISTEE, MICH.

Chapter 7
Fixing Old Photos That Are Too Light

The same thing goes for this chapter as the previous one. As I wrote this book, I began realizing that lighting issues accounted for the majority of problems with the old photos I had. Sure, we'll get into the rips and tears later, but the same thing holds true for old photos as it does for new ones. You've got to start with a well-exposed photo. If you don't start there, then all of the work you do to a photo will have less impact because people will inevitably concentrate on the fact that the photo is too bright or too dark.

Making Light Photos Darker

There are a lot of things that lead to our old photos becoming too light. It could be those photos were stored in a frame on a wall that was in sunlight all day, it could be the paper the photo was printed on, or it just could be the result of the camera technology 50 to 100 years ago. Whatever the cause, photos that are too light just don't look good, so I've got a few ways you can fix them.

METHOD 1: The Easy Way

This is the easy way. It works great if the entire photo is too light and you want a quick way to darken it.

STEP 1:

Open a light photo. By the way, you'll probably hear different terms for light photos. "Washed out" is a popular phrase. Whether "light" or "washed out," these photos just appear to lack detail altogether because they're either faded from time or overexposed in the first place.

STEP 2:

Duplicate the Background layer by pressing Ctrl-J (Mac: Command-J). This should leave you with two copies of the same photo in the Layers palette.

STEP 3:

Look in the top left of the Layers palette and you'll see the blend mode pop-up menu. By default, the layer's blend mode is set to Normal. Go ahead and expand this menu, and choose Multiply.

STEP 4:

This immediately darkens the photo and restores some detail and contrast back into the image.

TIP: Think of the Multiply blend mode as a darkening mode. Whenever you want to get rid of the lighter parts of a photo and make the dark parts even darker, try changing the layer blend mode to Multiply.

Continued

Fixing Old Photos That Are Too Light   *Chapter 7*

STEP 5:

If you find the photo is still not dark enough, try duplicating the top layer (the one you just set to Multiply). Press Ctrl-J (Mac: Command-J) to make another copy of the layer and it will retain the same Multiply blend mode and add even more detail and contrast to your photo. Try it two or three more times until you've got the photo to a point where you can see more of the details and it's not so washed out.

Before

After

SelectiveDarkening.jpg @ 100% (RGB/8)

CARL ZUMBANO

METHOD 2: When You Need More Control

This technique is a lifesaver when you need a little more control. For example, as you start to darken a lighter photo, you may inadvertently darken some areas you didn't want to.

Take a look at this example. I used the previous technique of duplicating the layer and changing the blend mode to Multiply. Notice how it severely darkened the dress at the bottom left of the photo. It's really too dark at this point. This technique lets you have a little more control over what gets darkened.

SelectiveDarkening.jpg @ 100% (Layer 1, RGB/8)

100%   7.667 inches x 12.153 inches (72 ppi)

Continued

STEP 1:

Here I've got a photo that already has some darker areas. If I were to darken the entire photo using the previous technique, then those areas would become too dark.

ShadowHighlight.jpg @ 50% (RGB/8)

WORKMAN FAMILY ARCHIVE

50%

STEP 2:

Go to the Enhance menu and choose Adjust Lighting>Shadows/Highlights.

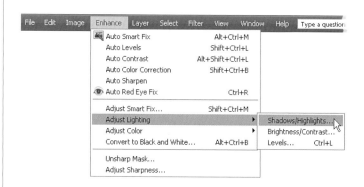

STEP 3:

The Shadows/Highlights adjustment dialog will open. This dialog works great for controlling the amount of darkening you add to an image because it looks at the light areas specifically and leaves the already dark areas alone.

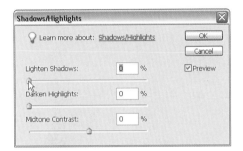

STEP 4:

Because we're not trying to lighten the photo, drag the Lighten Shadows slider all the way over to the left to 0%.

STEP 5:

Now start dragging the Darken Highlights slider toward the right. You don't want to go too far because you'll make the lighter areas (the sky in this photo) look too much like the dark areas. Somewhere around 40–50% usually works well, but feel free to push it higher if you have a really faded photo.

Continued

Fixing Old Photos That Are Too Light   *Chapter 7*

STEP 6:

Don't forget to finish this one up by trying to adjust the Midtone Contrast slider a bit toward the right. This will reduce some of the darkening that may have occurred to some of the already dark areas. A setting of +20–30% works well here.

Before

After

A lot of times people mistake a photo that lacks contrast for a photo that is too light. Frankly, it's really easy to do. Photos without much contrast are light as well, but in a different way. You can usually see the details and people in the photo, but you just can't see them very well. The photo will look very grayish overall and that just doesn't make for an interesting photo. The best way I can think of to describe this is that the photo looks very "blah" (that's a technical term by the way). There are a couple of easy ways to fix this though.

Improving Contrast in Old Photos

AddingContrast.jpg @ 50% (RGB/8)

WORKMAN FAMILY ARCHIVE

METHOD 1: The Easy Way

As you can imagine, there's an easy way to do this and a hard way. Let's take a look at the easy way first. Sometimes it works and sometimes it doesn't, but it's worth a try.

STEP 1:

Open a photo that is lacking contrast. These photos generally just look very bland to me. I can see the people in them but the lack of contrast causes the people to blend into everything around them.

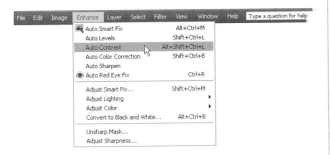

STEP 2:

Go under the Enhance menu and choose Auto Contrast, or press Ctrl-Alt-Shift-L (Mac: Command-Option-Shift-L).

Continued

STEP 3:

Elements will automatically try to fix the photo by boosting the contrast. As you can see, it looks much better than it did. The upside to this technique is that it's fast and definitely worth a try. The downside...you don't get any control, so if you're not happy or your photo needs some more work, then you're pretty much out of luck and you'll have to start over. If this one doesn't work for your photo, then read on because the next technique should do wonders for it.

METHOD 2: A Levels Adjustment

I have to say that I love this technique. It takes a photo that may have been a lost cause and turns it into something great.

STEP 1:

Try the same photo as we used in the first technique. This time, go under the Enhance menu and choose Adjust Lighting>Levels, or just press Ctrl-L (Mac: Command-L).

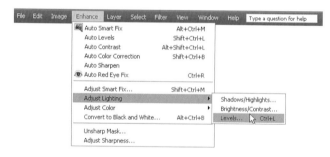

STEP 2:

This will open the Levels dialog. If you've been reading other tutorials in this book, then you'll know this adjustment pretty well. It's not only a great tool for lightening or darkening photos, but it works great for adding contrast as well.

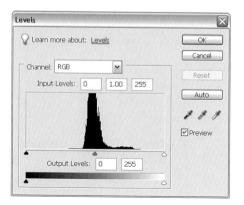

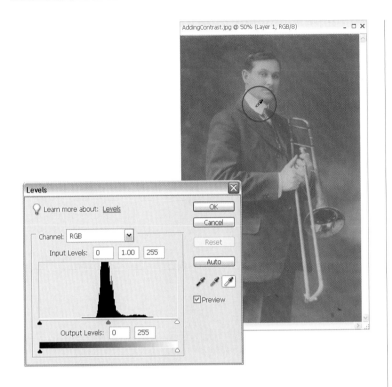

STEP 3:

First, click on the white highlights Eye-dropper on the right side of the dialog. Then click on something in the photo that should be white. Shirts work great, as in this example here. If there isn't anything white, then try clicking on the background or sky.

STEP 4:

That should immediately make the entire photo look drastically different, but better.

Continued

STEP 5:

To finish this off, take a look at the histogram in the dialog. If there are any areas on the far left or right sides that appear flat, like in this example, then drag the Input Levels slider on that side until it meets the mountainous area. Here, I'm dragging the black slider over to the right. This will add even more contrast to the photo.

TIP: When you're done with this tutorial, the photo may be too dark or too light. If so, then try the lightening or darkening techniques covered in this chapter and in Chapter 6.

After with Auto Contrast

Before

After with Levels adjustment

Darkening with Black and White

One way to work with old photos is to convert them to black and white first. This takes all of the guesswork about color out of the process and lets us concentrate on just black and white. And since most of the photos are black and white, or close to it anyway, you really don't lose anything. This technique works great for both darkening the photo and adding some great contrast, all at the same time.

STEP 1:

So far, we've looked at how to darken photos that are too light. We've also looked at how to add some contrast to light photos. Here we've got a photo that is both too light and that could use a contrast boost. This time though, we're going to use a technique that you probably wouldn't normally think of.

STEP 2:

Go to the Enhance menu and choose Convert to Black and White, or press Ctrl-Alt-B. This is a new feature in Elements 5 for converting color photos to black and white. It happens to work great for old photos as well.

STEP 3:
When the Convert to Black and White dialog opens, you'll see that all of the color is removed from the photo.

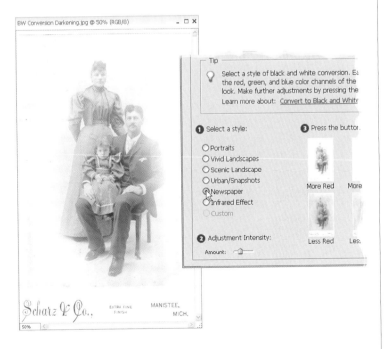

STEP 4:
In the dialog's Select a Style section, you'll see a few preset black-and-white conversions that you can click on to apply. I recommend clicking on all of them to see what they look like, but you'll most likely settle on my favorite for old photos—Newspaper. This automatically darkens the photo and adds a nice amount of contrast too.

Continued

Fixing Old Photos That Are Too Light

STEP 5:

Next, let's work on separating the people from the background a little more. Clicking on More Red, More Green, or More Blue in section 3 will lighten the entire photo. Since the people in the photo are what you're working on, their color will most likely fall into the red category, so click on More Red until that background becomes almost white. I did it twice for this photo.

TIP: If you were working on a scenic image with lots of blue sky or green grass, then you'd click on More Blue or More Green to lighten each respective color.

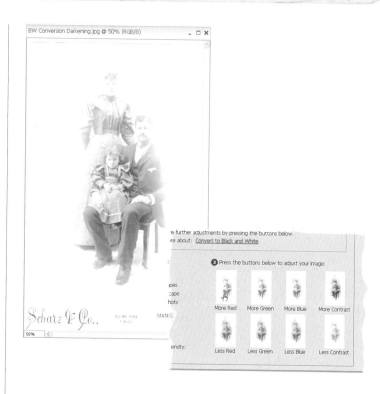

STEP 6:

Okay, at this point you should have the people darkened a bit and separated from the background pretty well. Now it's time to add some contrast to finish it off. Notice the More Contrast button at the bottom right of the dialog? Click on that two times to boost the contrast. Isn't that amazing? It almost makes the entire photo come to life. Click OK when you're done to apply the fix. Then sit back and think of how you just cheated Elements by using a dialog that was probably never intended for the purpose of fixing old photos to do a killer improvement of this one. Makes you feel like you got away with something, doesn't it? Don't worry, I won't tell.

TIP: If part of the photo is too light, like the gentleman's arm on the right side of this image, try using the next tutorial to darken that specific part.

Chapter 7   Fixing Old Photos That Are Too Light

Before

After

Darkening Specific Parts of a Photo

Many times, no matter what we do to darken a photo, certain areas in the photo are still just too light. When that happens, we need to take things a step further and work specifically on those areas to darken them.

STEP 1:

Open a photo that you've already tried to darken. Here I've used the techniques in this chapter to darken this photo. The overall photo looks fine but the facial features are just still too light.

Step 2:

First, click on the Create Adjustment Layer icon at the top of the Layers palette (it's the little half-black/half-white circle). Then choose Levels from the pop-up menu to add a Levels adjustment layer.

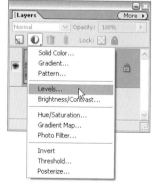

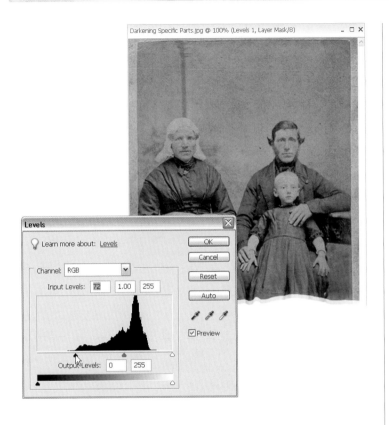

STEP 3:

In the Levels dialog, take the black Input Levels slider and move it over toward the right until the details in the face start becoming clearer. They may never be crystal clear because of the quality of the photo, but you can indeed make them darker than they were.

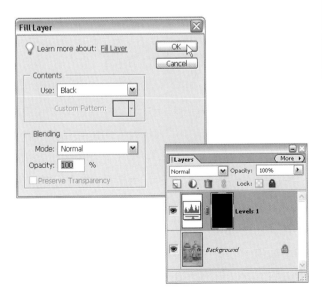

STEP 4:

Click OK to close the dialog. Now you'll have a Levels adjustment layer in the Layers palette, and you'll have a small white mask thumbnail right next to the adjustment layer thumbnail as well. Make sure the layer mask is active (you'll see a thin black frame around the corners), then go to the Edit menu and choose Fill Layer. From the Use pop-up menu, choose Black and click OK to fill that mask with black. This will totally hide the effects of the Levels adjustment you just added.

Continued

STEP 5:

Press B to select the Brush tool. Choose a small, soft-edged brush about the size of one of the people's eyes. Also, set the Opacity in the Options Bar to 100%.

STEP 6:

Press the letter D to set your Foreground color to white. Now start clicking on the eyes in the photo to paint with white. Notice how they start to darken and the detail becomes more apparent.

STEP 7:

Continue to click-and-paint on the facial features that you want to bring back. For the rest of the features here (mouths, noses), I set the Brush tool's opacity to 50%, so if you need to, you can set the opacity lower and click-and-paint on the same area several times to build the effect.

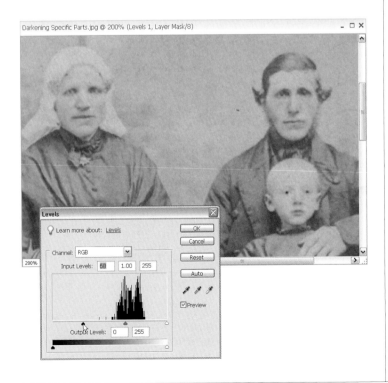

STEP 8:

When you're done, if the facial features are too dark or not dark enough, you can always double-click on the Levels adjustment layer in the Layers palette to reopen the dialog. Then move the black slider to see how it affects your image. Try moving the white slider to the left just a bit to add a little more contrast to those areas as well. It may help the blacks appear darker. This is a great way to finish off and see if you can pull any more detail out of those facial features.

Continued

Before

After

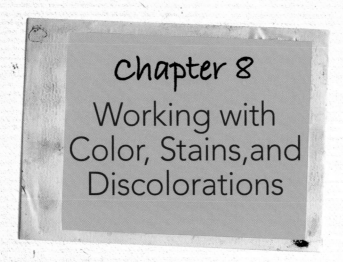

Chapter 8
Working with Color, Stains, and Discolorations

Well, you've almost made it to the last chapter. Or perhaps you just skipped right to this one. Either way, this chapter is all about color. After all, old photos may sit around for a long time. The paper they were printed on, the ink they were printed with, and the environment in which they were kept all contribute to changing the color of these photos over time. Here, we'll try a few ways to get that color looking right. We'll also take a look at specific discolorations, getting rid of textures on the paper, as well as breathing life into a black-and-white photo by adding color back into it.

Removing a Color Cast

Imagine the issues we face with color casts from today's photos. Well it can be even worse with old photos. Older photos are notorious for having a color cast or haze over them. They come in many colors and severity but I've got a few good ways to fix them.

METHOD 1: The Easy Way

This method is almost automatic. There's not much to it. Sometimes it works great and sometimes it doesn't. It's so simple though, that it's worth a try.

STEP 1:

Open a photo with a color cast. Here, I've got a photo of me in my kindergarten class. I can primarily see a red cast to it. (Psssst...can anyone pick me out in the photo?)

STEP 2:

Go under the Enhance menu and choose Adjust Color>Adjust Color for Skin Tone. This will open the Adjust Color for Skin Tone dialog.

STEP 3:

The only thing you really have to do here is click on the skin of someone in the photo. Here I've chosen the little boy next to the girl in the flowery dress. Now just click on his skin somewhere. I usually choose the forehead for a good skin color.

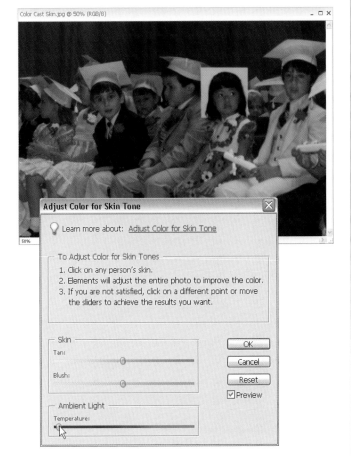

STEP 4:

Elements will automatically adjust the photo. Here, it took away the red color cast and made the photo slightly bluish, but better than it was. If it's too cool (aka: blue), then try adjusting the Temperature slider at the bottom of the dialog by moving it slightly (and I mean slightly) to the right. Go ahead and click OK when you're done. Oh yeah, did you find me yet?

Continued

Before

After

METHOD 2: A Levels Adjustment

This one works great when the first one doesn't. It requires a little more work, but the results can look great.

CARLINE ZUMBANO

STEP 1:

Open another photo that has a color cast to it. As you can see, this one has a heavy greenish/yellow haze to it.

STEP 2:

This time, go under the Enhance menu to Adjust Lighting>Levels, or press Ctrl-L (Mac: Command-L). This will open the Levels dialog.

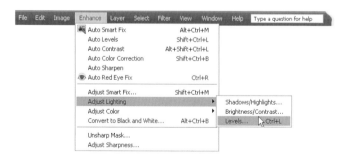

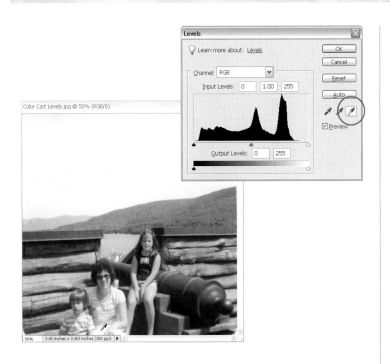

STEP 3:

Click once on the white point Eyedropper in the center right to select it. Then click on an area of the photo that looks like it should be white. Here, I'm guessing that my mother's pants are probably white, so I'll click on them. The difference is extremely noticeable once I click. By the way, guess who she's holding? I was a cute little guy, wasn't I?

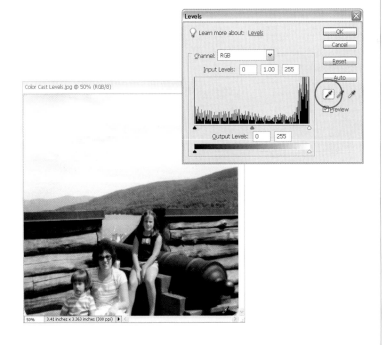

STEP 4:

Now do the same with the black point Eyedropper. Click on it and then click on something in the photo that should be black. Here, I'll click on a shadow area under the cannon. That adds some nice contrast to the photo as well.

Continued

STEP 5:

You're pretty much done. If the photo is too dark or too light, go ahead and try adjusting the middle gray slider under the histogram a little. Not too much though, but a small move to the left or right can do a nice job in lightening or darkening the photo.

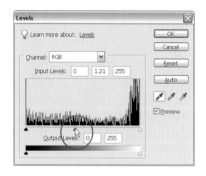

Before

After

Color Cast Variations.jpg @ 50% (RGB/8)

CARLINE ZUMBANO

50%   3.26 inches x 4.643 inches (300 ppi)

METHOD 3: Color Variations

This one is a little more advanced, but you get plenty of control along with it.

STEP 1:
Open another photo with a color cast to it. As you can see, this problem is prevalent, as I have many of these photos to demonstrate with. Here, we've got a photo with a green cast to it.

STEP 2:
Go to Enhance>Adjust Color>Color Variations. This will open the Color Variations dialog.

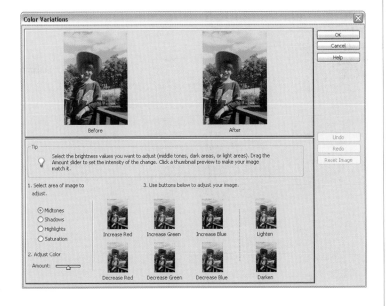

Color Variations

OK
Cancel
Help

Before   After

Undo
Redo
Reset Image

Tip

Select the brightness values you want to adjust (middle tones, dark areas, or light areas). Drag the Amount slider to set the intensity of the change. Click a thumbnail preview to make your image match it.

1. Select area of image to adjust.

3. Use buttons below to adjust your image.

- ⦿ Midtones
- ◯ Shadows
- ◯ Highlights
- ◯ Saturation

Increase Red   Increase Green   Increase Blue   Lighten

2. Adjust Color

Amount:

Decrease Red   Decrease Green   Decrease Blue   Darken

Continued

Working with Color, Stains, and Discolorations   **Chapter 8**   205

STEP 3:

Remember back in Chapter 1 when we looked at the ways we can neutralize color casts or hazes? Well, the same principles apply here. For example, the color cast here is primarily green. If you don't believe me, try going to the Filter menu under Blur>Average. This filter creates one color that is the average of all colors in the photo. It looks pretty darn green to me.

STEP 4:

Press Ctrl-Z (Mac: Command-Z) to Undo. Now that we've identified the color cast, we can use a color that is opposite it on the color wheel to fix the photo—in this example, red.

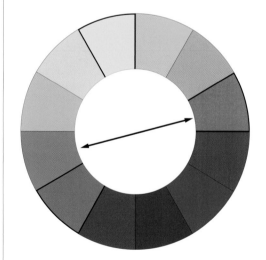

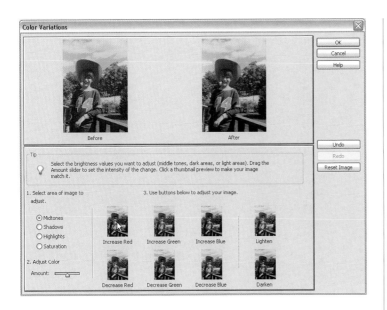

STEP 5:

Okay, back to the Color Variations dialog. Notice how there are three colors listed and each has an Increase and Decrease thumbnail associated with it? By clicking Increase Red, we're essentially telling Elements to add—you guessed it—more red color to the photo. So, try clicking on it twice. Keep an eye on the Before and After previews at the top.

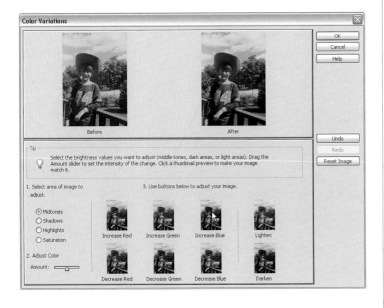

STEP 6:

It's looking better so far. However, it's looking a little too red for my taste, so I'm going to click on Increase Blue once as well, to offset the red a bit.

Continued

STEP 7:

Great. You can also move the Amount slider at the bottom left of the dialog. This affects the intensity of the colors you're clicking on in the middle. So, for example, if I reduce the Amount slider and click on Increase Blue, I still get more blue in the photo but not as much as I would have if I left the slider in the middle. Feel free to continue to adjust the color for your own photo. I think we've neutralized the color cast pretty well here, so I'm just going to click OK to close the dialog.

TIP: You can always try to mix and match these three techniques. For example, try the Color Variations technique, and then try following it up with the quick Levels adjustment we used in Method 2. Remember, as Ansel Adams once said, "There are no rules for good photographs, there are only good photographs." Use whatever works, and if combining two of these techniques gives you a nice-colored photo, then go for it.

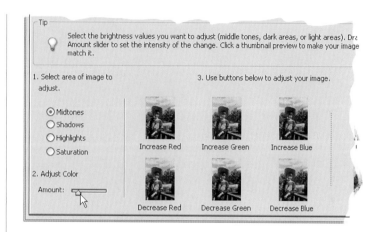

Before

After

Adding Color to Black-and-White Photos

As you may have seen so far, there are plenty of things that we can do to restore old photos. However, none of them really breathes life into an old photo like adding color to it does.

STEP 1:

First open a photo to colorize. This technique requires that a photo be in the RGB Color mode to work. Since many old black-and-white photos start out as grayscale, take a look in your image's title bar to see if it says "Gray" in it. If so, read Step 2. If not, skip to Step 3.

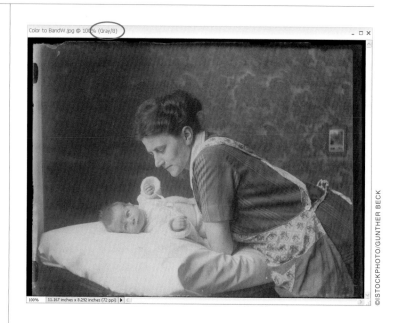

STEP 2:

If your title bar does say "Gray," then your image is in Grayscale mode. No worries though, to change this just go to the Image menu to Mode and choose RGB Color. See, that was easy, wasn't it? Now you're ready to move on.

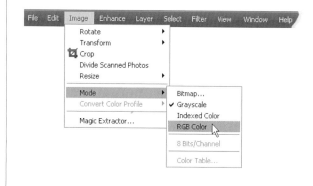

WORKMAN FAMILY ARCHIVE

STEP 3:

The other thing you may run into is if your old photo has, well, that "old photo" look to it. This technique really requires that the photo be just black and white. If your photo looks like this, then try the next tutorial to get rid of that old photo look.

STEP 4:

Okay, now we're ready to start. First, let's work on the skin since that's one of the most important parts. Click on the Create a New Layer icon at the top of the Layers palette to create a new blank layer above the Background layer. Double-click on the layer's name to rename it and call it "Skin."

STEP 5:

Open another color photo that has some people in it. We're going to sample the skin color, so we have something to work from. Select the Eyedropper tool (I) and click once on the skin to set your Foreground color to the skin color. You can close the color photo now.

Continued

STEP 6:

Click once on the Skin layer to select it. Then press B to select the Brush tool from the Toolbox. Choose a smaller, soft-edged brush and start painting over the skin areas in the photo. Yes, I know it looks really bad at this point, but bear with me.

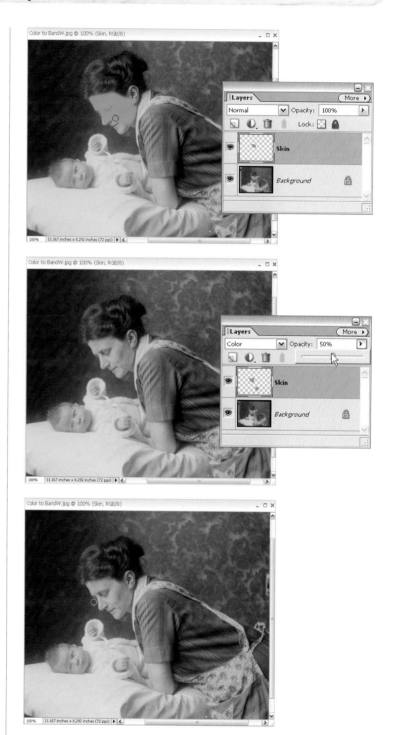

STEP 7:

Once you're done painting over the skin, change the layer's blend mode (in the top left of the Layers palette) from Normal to Color. This mode shows the underlying details from the original photo (shadows and highlights), but tries to keep the color of the layer you just painted at the same time. It's almost like tinting the black and white. Also, set the Opacity setting to around 50–60% to reduce the intensity.

STEP 8:

Now you can see the details under the color. Cool, huh? If you need to add any areas, just use the Brush tool to continue adding skin tone to the photo. If you mess up, just press the letter E to switch to the Eraser tool and erase away those areas that don't belong.

STEP 9:

Now let's work on her hair, since the people are really the most important parts of the photo here. First, create a new blank layer just like we did in Step 4. Name this layer "Hair."

STEP 10:

Again, open another photo and use the Eyedropper tool to sample the person's hair. This works best if you know what color hair the person in the old photo had, so try to ask around in your family (or a client if you're doing this for business purposes) to see what the original color was.

STEP 11:

Click once on the Hair layer to select it. Back in Steps 6 and 7, we actually painted first and then changed the layer's blend mode to Color. This time, try changing the blend mode to Color first.

Continued

STEP 12:

Now, press B to select the Brush tool and start painting on the hair. When you're done, you may want to reduce the opacity of the layer depending on how intense the hair color looks. Somewhere between 40–60% works well here.

STEP 13:

Okay, now let's move to the dress. Create a new blank layer named "Dress" to hold the dress color. Change the blend mode from Normal to Color.

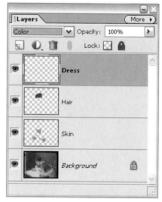

STEP 14:

Click on the Foreground color swatch at the bottom of the Toolbox to bring up the Color Picker, and set your Foreground color to a blue color. I used R:118, G:173, B:255 here.

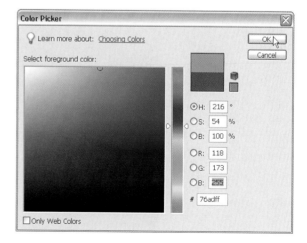

STEP 15:

Start painting with the Brush tool on the dress to add some color. Remember, if you add paint outside the lines of the dress, you can always press E to switch to the Eraser tool and erase away those areas.

STEP 16:

After you paint certain colors, you may think that another color would look better. Here's a great trick, so you don't have to go recoloring the whole area again. Click once on the layer that holds the color you'd like to change (in this case, the dress). Press Ctrl-U (Mac: Command-U) to open the Hue/Saturation dialog.

STEP 17:

Adjust the Hue slider until you get the color that you are looking for. Always adjust the Saturation slider to make the color more or less intense. Finally, adjust the Lightness slider to make the color lighter or darker. When you do it this way, you can have total control over the color you've painted even after you've painted it. It saves a lot of time so you don't have to go back and repaint the whole thing if you decide to change colors.

Continued

STEP 18:

Finish the photo by creating a new layer for each area and adding color separately to each layer. When you're done, you may have a lot of layers but it's worth it in case you decide to change your mind and switch colors.

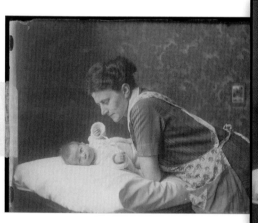

Before

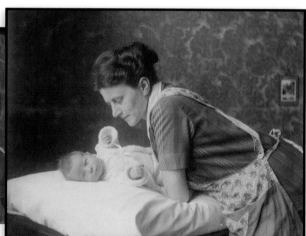

After

Read the title to this tutorial and you'll probably know exactly what I mean. You know, that "old photo" look. You see, I can't explain it. There is just a look to old photos that makes them look, well...old. They have a yellowish/brownish color to them from being exposed to the elements for 80 years and it's not very appealing. Let's take a look at how to remove it here.

Getting Rid of That "Old Photo" Look

STEP 1:
Open an old photo that has that "old photo" look to it. Trust me, you'll know it when you see it. By the way, if you were thinking of that yellowish color tint that photos from the '70s tend to have, then you're probably not alone. While this tutorial concentrates mostly on those *really* old photos, take a look at the first tutorial in this chapter for three ways to fix the color in those '70s photos.

STEP 2:
Go to the Enhance menu and choose Adjust Color>Remove Color, or press Ctrl-Shift-U (Mac: Command-Shift-U). This will take all of the color from the photo.

Continued

STEP 3:

Now let's add some contrast back into the photo. You can use the tutorial in Chapter 7 on page 183 for this or try the quick and dirty way under Enhance>Auto Contrast. There you have it. The old look is basically gone. You could stop here if you're happy, but read on if you want a different way to finish this off.

STEP 4:

Many people tend to like the sepia tint that those old photos have. You see, that old photo look I was talking about tends to make everything look like a dull, brown mess—even the details in the photo. That's why we converted it to black and white, and boosted the contrast a little. That makes the overall tone of the photo much better. However, I personally like the sepia tint, but I just don't like the aged look of the original. I'm much happier when I can control the sepia tone, instead of it being forced on me as it was in the original. So, let's add our own. Go to the top of the Layers palette and click on the Create Adjustment Layer icon. Select Hue/Saturation from the pop-up menu that appears.

STEP 5:

In the Hue/Saturation dialog, click the Colorize checkbox in the bottom-right corner to turn it on. Then take the Hue slider and drag it to 34. That should add a nice sepia color to the photo.

STEP 6:

The best part about it is that you have control. You can change the color by adjusting the Hue slider. You can also change the saturation, or how strong the color is, by adjusting the Saturation slider. Notice how much richer the blacks are than the original photo was. Both versions have a brown color tint, but the Hue/Saturation version pops out much more.

Before

After

Removing Paper Patterns and Textures

When you look closely at older photos, you'll notice that many of the papers they were printed on have a certain pattern or texture to them. It's usually not so bad when you're looking at the real photo. However, once you scan that photo into your computer, those paper textures and patterns become a problem. Especially if you need to restore the photo, because now you not only have to worry about the details of the photo but you also need to keep the same paper texture. So, why not remove the texture altogether?

STEP 1:

Here, I've opened a photo I scanned using my favorite scanner in the world, the Epson Perfection V750-M PRO. It's so good that it actually picks up the texture on the paper.

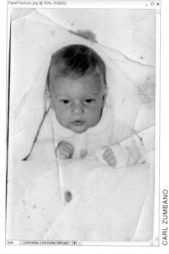

STEP 2:

Double-click the Zoom tool in the Toolbox to set your zoom percentage to 100%. This shows us exactly how the image looks when blown up to full size.

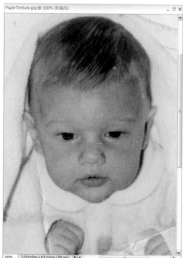

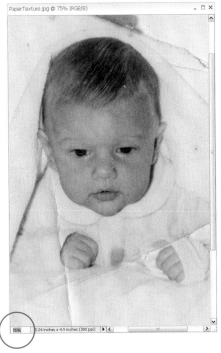

STEP 3:

Let's start zooming out until we don't see the texture anymore. Double-click in the bottom-left field under your image to highlight the text that reads "100%." Then type 75 and press the Enter (Mac: Return) key to zoom out to 75%. I can still see the texture, so go ahead and enter 50% and press the Enter key.

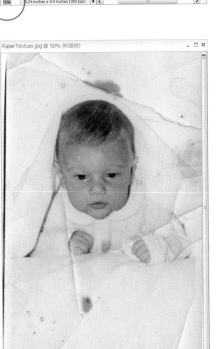

STEP 4:

The texture is pretty much gone in the 50% view, so make a mental note of the percentage at which it disappears.

Continued

STEP 5:

Now, go to the Image menu and choose Resize>Image Size, or press Ctrl-Alt-I (Mac: Command-Option-I). When the Image Size dialog opens, make sure both the Resample Image and Constrain Proportions checkboxes are turned on at the bottom left of the dialog. In the Pixel Dimensions section, choose Percent from the Width and Height pop-up menus. Actually, you should just need to change one and the other will change automatically.

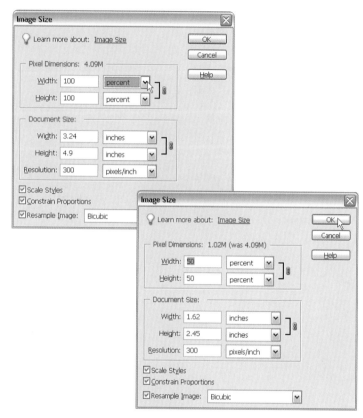

STEP 6:

Then, in the Width field, type in whatever percentage it was from Step 4 that made the texture disappear. The Height field should change automatically. In this case, I entered 50%. Press OK and the image will be resized.

STEP 7:

Now, double-click on the Zoom tool again in the Toolbox to set the image view to 100%. You should no longer see the texture, and the photo should look just like it did in Step 4 when the texture disappeared.

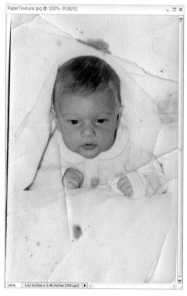

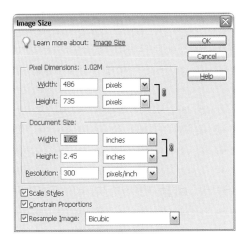

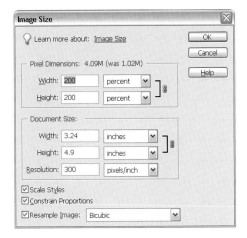

STEP 8:

However, by resizing you've also made the image half its size. At this point, you need to make a decision. Go back to the Image Size dialog or just press Ctrl-Alt-I (Mac: Command-Option-I) to open it. Under Document Size, look at the Width and Height fields (they should be in inches; if not, choose Inches from the pop-up menus to the right of these fields) and see what they read. Decide for yourself if you'll want to print the photo out at a larger size than this. At this point, the document size could be fine and you're done with the tutorial. The texture is gone and everyone is happy, right?

STEP 9:

If, however, the document size is too small and you need it back to the size it was before you resized in Step 6, then you need to do one more thing. While still in the Image Size dialog, change pixels to percent once again in the Pixel Dimensions section. Then use this formula to get the image back to the original size:

(100/percentage used in Step 4) x 100%

In this case, it would be: (100/50 = 2) x 100 = 200%. So, I would enter 200% for the Width and Height settings. Had I used 75% in Step 4 then it would be: (100/75 = 1.33) x 100 = 133%. I promise this is the most math that you'll have to do in the entire book.

Continued

STEP 10:

Okay, now press OK once you've entered your percentage. The photo is resized and will print out at the same size it would have when you first opened the image. If you still think there is too much texture, press Ctrl-J (Mac: Command-J) to duplicate the Background layer. Then press R to get the Blur tool, choose a soft-edged brush, and make sure the Strength is set to 50% up in the Options Bar.

STEP 11:

With your new layer active, start painting with the Blur tool on the areas that have too much texture. Be careful to avoid any detail areas, such as the eyes and the mouth in the photo shown here. Since your brush is set to 50%, you can always paint a second time to build up the effect.

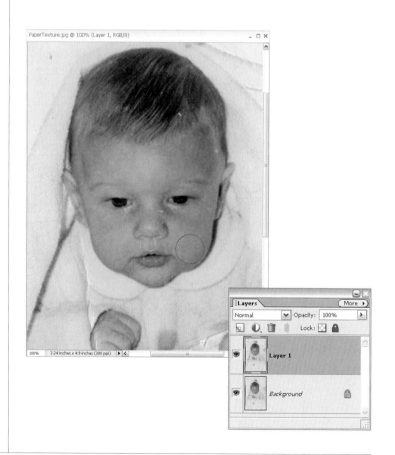

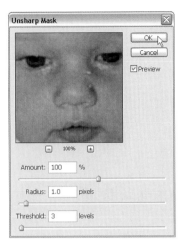

STEP 12:

Now, some may argue that the photo may not be quite as sharp as it was in the beginning. If you're not one of them and you think it looks fine, then by all means skip this part. But, if you do notice any blurring of the photo, you can fix it by choosing Enhance>Unsharp Mask to sharpen the photo (in Elements versions 3 and 4, Unsharp Mask is under Filter>Sharpen>Unsharp Mask—it's the same filter, though). Enter an Amount setting of 100, Radius of 1 and Threshold of 3. Click OK and that'll sharpen the photo to help offset any blurring effect we may have had when increasing the size of the image.

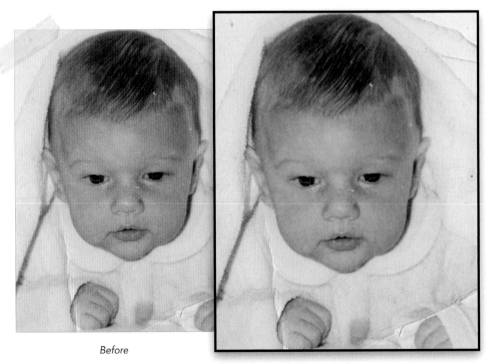

Before

After

Repairing Water Damage

After Hurricane Katrina hit in 2005, many families lost everything—homes, cars, furniture, electronics, and even their family photos. Insurance companies hopefully cover the material losses, but you can't put a price on losing memories. Fortunately, many folks rushed to the aid of those affected through a website called Operation Photo Rescue—a worldwide network of volunteers dedicated to trying to restore lost photos (mostly water damaged, in this case). Many of the techniques they use work perfectly in Elements, so let's take a look at how to fix some water damage.

STEP 1:

Open a photo with some water damage. Here, I've got a photo of one of our graphic designers, Jessica, who worked on this book. Isn't she cute? However, you can see some pretty severe water damage through many parts of the photo.

PELUSO FAMILY ARCHIVE

STEP 2:

The first thing is to try to locate other photos that are similar to this one. I'm a big fan of Katrin Eismann and her retouching and restoration methods. She often tells people to beg, borrow, or steal from wherever they can to repair a photo, and I think that advice works perfectly here. Here I've got a scan of a few other shots of the same girl, and some of them include parts that we can utilize to fix our photo—namely the bottom of the dress near the feet.

PELUSO FAMILY ARCHIVE

STEP 3:

First, go to the photo that has the parts you want to steal. Press L to select the Lasso tool and draw a selection around that area. It's okay to select more than you need, as we can always erase it later.

STEP 4:

Press Ctrl-C (Mac: Command-C) to Copy this area from the source photo. Then click on the photo that you want to repair to move it to the front and press Ctrl-V (Mac: Command-V) to Paste the copied area in. You'll see that it gets placed on a new layer above the original photo.

Continued

STEP 5:

Press V to select the Move tool and move the new piece into place. You can always drop the opacity of the copied layer so you can see behind it and line it up correctly.

TIP: If your photos are different sizes, then press Ctrl-T (Mac: Command-T) to go into Free Transform mode. You can not only resize the copied area, but you can rotate it as well to help it fit correctly.

STEP 6:

You'll notice that some areas just don't fit in. To fix this, press E to select the Eraser tool and choose one of the soft-edged brushes from the Brush Picker in the Options Bar. Start clicking-and-painting to erase in areas that don't match up. If you go too far, then just press Ctrl-Z (Mac: Command-Z) to go back and try again.

PELUSO FAMILY ARCHIVE

STEP 7:

Now, we need to fix the rest of the area around the dress. You've got a couple options here: first, if you can beg, borrow, or steal from another photo, then that's the ideal method because it's usually less work. Or, you can try the "Don't Fix the Background—Move the Person" tutorial in Chapter 9 to move your subject to a brand new background. For my example, there is a background in another photo that isn't damaged, so I'm going to select the Lasso tool from the Toolbox again and quickly select it.

TIP: If you do use the tutorial in Chapter 9 to change your background, keep in mind that your background color may not always match the one I used in the tutorial. A great trick is to follow the tutorial as stated to create the black-and-white background. Then go to Enhance>Adjust Color>Adjust Hue/Saturation and change the Hue setting. Be sure to turn on the Colorize checkbox in that dialog as well, so you can change colors to fit your photo.

STEP 8:

Then, just like Step 4, copy-and-paste the background selection into the image you're working on. Use the Move tool to position it into place and use the Eraser tool to erase away the areas that don't fit. This takes care of most of the damage I had in the background, but it'll typically still leave the edges of the people with some water damage—the chances that the person in the undamaged photo is in the same pose and spot as the damaged photo are pretty slim.

Continued

STEP 9:

For the remaining areas, I'm going to click on the Create a New Layer icon at the top of the Layers palette to create a new blank layer. First, press Ctrl-+ (Mac: Command-+; plus sign) to zoom in to the area that needs to be fixed. Select the Clone Stamp tool (with the Sample All Layers checkbox turned on in the Options Bar) and Alt-click (Mac: Option-click) in a clean area of the background.

STEP 10:

Then, while you're still zoomed in, start to fill in those areas of water damage in the background. Typically, they'll be around the edges of the people since that's the area hardest to get perfect with Step 8. As you get closer to the edges of the dress, you'll probably want to switch to a harder-edged brush in the Brush Picker (those are the brushes with the very crisp edges, not the soft ones). That'll help you keep that clean edge between the person in the photo and the background.

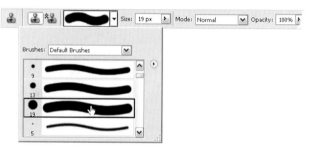

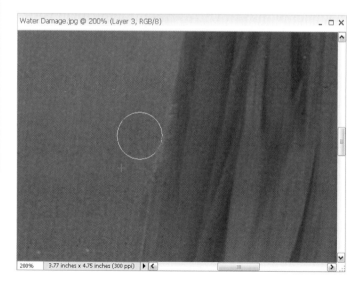

Before

After

Repair for Grandpa's birthday album!

Chapter 9

Rebuilding
Techniques

Here's where we get to the meat
of restoration. Once you've got the exposure
(lights and darks) of the photo looking good,
it's time to bring in the heavy artillery. I have no
idea why I brought military-speak into this, but it
just seemed appropriate. Anyway, in this chapter
we're going to concentrate on rebuilding techniques.
These range from repairing rips, tears, bends, and
folds to adding missing people back into a photo.
It's amazing how the tools here in Elements can truly
help you restore (and even create) those lost memories
from the past.

Removing Dust and Specks

Dust and specks on our photos are inevitable. These spots show their signs mostly when we scan photos into the computer (covered in the Appendix). The light from the scanner accentuates any little texture or spot on the photo. There are a few ways to fix this, and we'll take a look at the pros and cons of them here.

METHOD 1: The Easy Way

This one is really simple. However, sometimes it blurs the photo too much depending on how many times you have to run this filter. Let's take a look:

STEP 1:

Open a photo that has tiny spots on it. These spots could be dust, small scratches, specks, or just about anything else. You'll know them when you see them.

WORKMAN FAMILY ARCHIVE

STEP 2:

Go to the Filter menu and choose Noise>Despeckle.

STEP 3:

You don't get any dialogs here. This filter basically looks at the edges in the photo and tries to keep them intact. Then it blurs everything else.

STEP 4:

If running this filter once doesn't do it for you, then you can try it several times. Just press Ctrl-F (Mac: Command-F) to rerun the previously used filter. You can press it a few times and as you can see, it does a pretty good job of removing those little specks. Here I reran the Despeckle filter about five times. You may need to rerun the filter a few more times on your own photos.

Before

After

Continued

METHOD 2: Controlling the Blurriness

The problem with the previous method is that it blurs your photo each time you run the filter. Some photos can handle it without showing the blurriness, but some can't. Here's another example of the photo used with Method 1. In order to completely get rid of all the specks, the Despeckle filter had to be used eight times. The specks are gone, but the photo is pretty blurry. Read on for another technique that can help reduce that:

STEP 1:

Let's try this technique using the same photo from the previous tutorial. This time, go under the Filter menu and choose Noise>Dust and Scratches.

STEP 2:

When the dialog opens, you'll see that you have two settings to adjust. The first setting, Radius, determines how much blur you're going to add to this photo in order to remove those specks. I keep a *very* low setting here. Usually, 1 pixel will do just fine. Anything higher will blur the image too much.

STEP 3:

The Threshold setting is almost like an Opacity slider here. If you keep it at 0 levels, then you're telling Elements to apply the full fixing amount it can (with only 1 pixel as a Radius) to the photo. If you raise it higher, then you apply less of a fix to the photo but you'll also blur it less. When you're done, click OK to apply the fix to the photo.

TIP: The two adjustments can seem a little confusing here. I go about it like this: First I set the Radius setting to 1 (2 if it's a *really* bad photo, but I rarely do that). Then I adjust the Threshold slider. I start by setting it all the way over to the right at 255. Then I start dragging the slider to the left until my specks disappear.

Before

After

Fixing Minor Tears and Creases

Tears happen for a number of reasons. It could be that someone inadvertently tore the photo. More often, it happens from the photo being bent repeatedly. Eventually, the bent area may become separated enough from the rest of the photo to tear, and it causes a pretty unsightly appearance. With a little cloning though, we can fix it and bring it back to life.

STEP 1:

Open a photo that has a tear in it. Here, you can see a few tears that most likely occurred from the photo being repeatedly bent.

STEP 2:

Press S to select the Clone Stamp tool. In the Options Bar, choose a soft-edged brush from the Brush Picker with a size that is smaller than the crack. Also, make sure that the Sample All Layers checkbox is turned on.

WORKMAN FAMILY ARCHIVE

STEP 3:

Remember how we turned on Sample All Layers in the previous step? Now, go ahead and click on the Create a New Layer icon at the top of the Layers palette to create a new blank layer. This blank layer, along with the Sample All Layers checkbox we turned on, lets us use a separate layer to hold our repairs. That way we don't harm the original photo.

STEP 4:

Let's work on the tears away from the face for now, since they're pretty easy to fix. Press Z and click on the photo to zoom in on a tear, then press S to return to the Clone Stamp tool. Press-and-hold the Alt (Mac: Option) key and click in a clean area of the photo without any tears. Make sure you Alt-click close to the torn area, though. Elements is going to sample from there when we fix the photo, and we don't want the area it samples from to be too far from the original.

STEP 5:

Now, click over part of the tear. Notice that Elements is using the area you sampled from and is painting it over the tear wherever you click. At this point, I usually just click a few times to see how it looks. If you start painting large strokes, you run the risk of creating a repeating pattern and that's a dead giveaway that your photo was repaired.

Continued

STEP 6:

Continue to click-and-paint over the tear a few times. Keep an eye on the little crosshair next to your brush. That is showing you where Elements is sampling from (you can see it on the chair back here).

STEP 7:

If that crosshair starts moving over an area that doesn't look like the area you want to fix, it's time to Undo (press Ctrl-Z [Mac: Command-Z]) and press-and-hold the Alt (Mac: Option) key to sample from another area. Again, start clicking to paint over the tear. As I mentioned earlier, save the face for last.

STEP 8:

When you get near the chair, work on each chair rung individually. Press-and-hold the Alt (Mac: Option) key to sample an area just above what you want to fix.

STEP 9:

As you move into larger areas, you can experiment with painting broader strokes. Instead of just clicking with the Clone Stamp tool, try clicking-and-dragging along the tear. If you sampled from a good spot near your tear, you may get away with a nice long stroke and fix a large area quickly. Also, resize the brush as needed (as the size of the tear increases or decreases) using the Left and Right Bracket keys.

STEP 10:

Paint downward with the Clone Stamp tool with quick clicks. If you paint too far downward without lifting your mouse button, you'll start to lose your sample point. Click-and-move your cursor and click again to rebuild the chair piece-by-piece.

STEP 11:

If working with the Clone Stamp tool gets a little tedious, you can always try the Spot Healing Brush (J). Make sure the Sample All Layers checkbox is turned on in the Options Bar and just click to paint over some of the torn areas. It's not as reliable as the Clone Stamp tool, but it may do the job for areas without a lot of detail in them.

Continued

Rebuilding Techniques   *Chapter 9*   241

STEP 12:

Okay, at this point you should have fixed everything but the face. So let's set our sights on that area. Press the letter Z for the Zoom tool and click to zoom in, so only the face fills the entire screen.

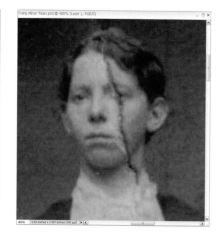

STEP 13:

Press L to select the Lasso tool. Drag a quick selection around the eye area of the face that isn't torn.

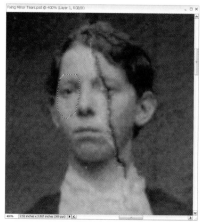

STEP 14:

Go under the Edit menu and choose Copy Merged to not only copy the contents of the layer you have selected, but everything that is inside the selection, regardless of what layer it's on.

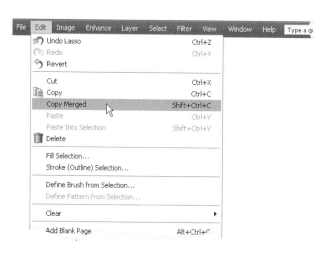

STEP 15:

Then press Ctrl-V (Mac: Command-V) to Paste the copied area. You'll see a new layer appear in the Layers palette.

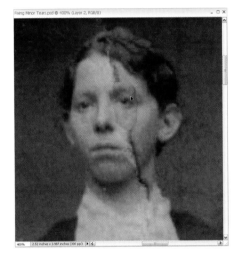

STEP 16:

Click once on that new layer to select it. Then, go to Image>Rotate>Flip Layer Horizontal. Press V to select the Move tool and move the copied eye and face over to the other side.

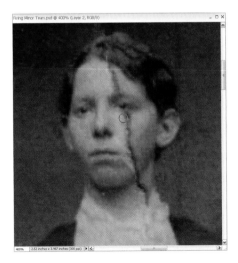

STEP 17:

Press E to select the Eraser tool from the Toolbox. Use a small brush and start erasing away everything but the duplicate eye.

Continued

STEP 18:

It's looking pretty good, but the eye is just a little small. If you notice, her head is slightly turned which changes the perspective of the two eyes. Let's make this one larger by going to Image>Transform>Free Transform (or just press Ctrl-T [Mac: Command-T]). Then drag the middle-right handle out toward the side of the head just a bit until it fills the eye area. Click the green checkmark beneath the bounding box to commit the transformation (or just press the Enter [Mac: Return] key).

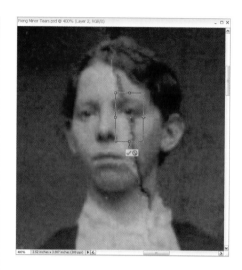

STEP 19:

Well, we've repaired just about everything. The last thing to do is use the Clone Stamp tool on the face for the rest of the area we weren't able to duplicate in the previous steps. I suggest zooming way in and resampling often here, because you want to try to match the skin as close as possible with the skin around it.

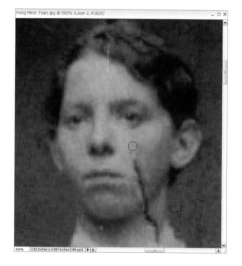

Before

After

Piecing Together a Torn Photo

I was sitting here one evening reviewing my outline for the book and looking through photos to decide which tutorials to include. Right in front of me was a torn-in-half photo of my great-grandparents. I decided to restore it (not even thinking about the book) and put it back together. I finished fixing it and went back to deciding what tutorials to include. I know what you're thinking: Why not turn what I had just done into a tutorial? Well, I'm not that sharp. It took about 10 minutes, but it did eventually click, so here it is.

STEP 1:

Here I've scanned in the pieces of my torn photo using the Epson Perfection V750-M PRO. It's a great scanner and it gives you a very high-quality start from which to restore your photos.

TIP: When you're scanning the photo pieces, make sure you leave ample space between them. I suggest at least a half-inch to make things easier later.

STEP 2:

Select the Magic Wand tool (W) from the Toolbox and make sure the Tolerance is set to 32 in the Options Bar. Click on the white background area of the scanner bed to select it.

STEP 3:

Now, instead of selecting the scanner bed, I want to select the photo pieces. So, just choose Select>Inverse to select everything but the white scanner bed area. Don't deselect yet.

STEP 4:

I want to put the pieces of the photo onto separate layers. With the marching ants still active, press the L key to select the Lasso tool. Press-and-hold the Alt (Mac: Option) key and you'll see a little minus sign next to your Lasso tool cursor. This means you'll be subtracting from the selection. Go ahead and click-and-drag a rough selection around the large piece of the photo to deselect it.

Continued

STEP 5:

Now you should only have the torn piece of the photo selected. Go to the Layer menu and choose New>Layer via Cut to move this piece up onto its own layer. You should now have two layers in the Layers palette.

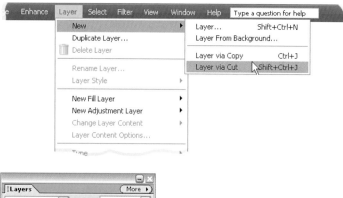

STEP 6:

It's now time to position the layer where it belongs. Click once on the top layer (the smaller piece of the photo) to select it and then press Ctrl-T (Mac: Command-T) to go into Free Transform mode. You'll see a rectangular bounding box appear around the object.

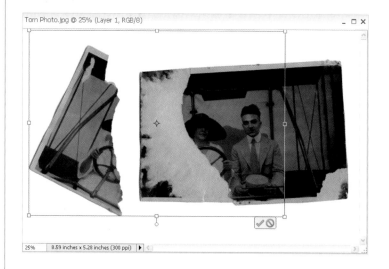

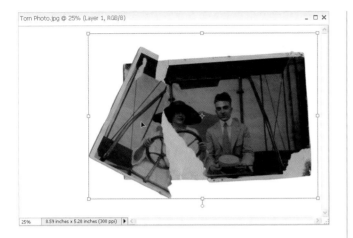

STEP 7:

Put your cursor inside the bounding box and move the piece over toward the other photo piece.

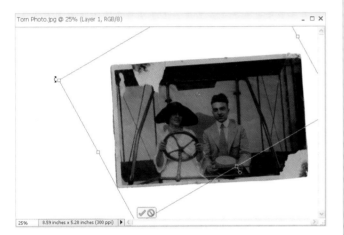

STEP 8:

Now move your cursor outside the box and it will change to a little, curved two-sided arrow. Click-and-drag in a counter-clockwise direction to rotate the piece into place. Feel free to move and rotate it a few times until you get it just right. Click the green checkmark at the bottom of the bounding box when you're done to commit the transformation (or just press the Enter [Mac: Return] key).

STEP 9:

Okay, at this point we could go on and fix the tear in the photo, but bear with me for a second. First, press V to select the Move tool and move the torn piece over to the right a bit so it's over the larger photo piece.

Continued

STEP 10:

Press Z for the Zoom tool and click to zoom in on the right edge of the smaller torn piece. Notice the small white fringe around the edge?

STEP 11:

We can leave that white fringe and just clone it out later, but it'll be a lot easier if we can get rid of it now. Go under the Enhance menu to Adjust Color>Defringe Layer (this is not available in Elements 3).

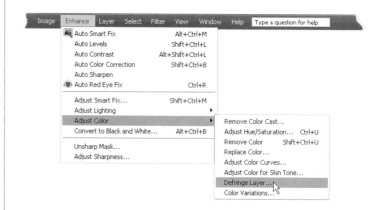

STEP 12:

Enter 2 pixels for the Width setting and click OK. Watch closely and you should see that little white fringe disappear for the most part. This will really help the cloning process, since you'll have less junk to contend with.

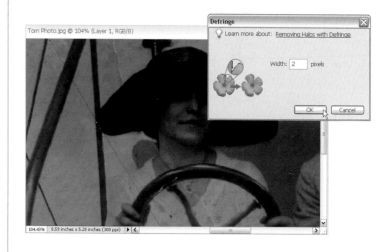

STEP 13:

Okay, now move the smaller photo piece back into place and you're ready to repair the tear in the photo. First, click on the Create a New Layer icon at the top of the Layers palette to create a new blank layer to hold your changes.

STEP 14:

Use the Clone Stamp tool (S) just like you did in the "Fixing Minor Tears and Creases" tutorial earlier in this chapter to fix the seam between the two pieces, along with other torn areas. Here, I also used the Crop tool (C) to crop, rotate, and straighten the photo.

Before

After

Repairing Bends or Cracks in Photos

If you bend an old photo enough, you're bound to leave some permanent damage. Many times those bends result in tears in the paper because it becomes so fragile, but sometimes it just leaves an ugly, white line across the photo. There are a few ways to fix this. I've got a really easy one if the photo happens to be bent in the right location. If not, then I'll show you another way that requires a little more work.

METHOD 1: The Easy Way

This one works great if you have a bend or crack in the photo that is fairly straight and doesn't spider out from the main bend too far.

STEP 1:

Open a bent photo. In this example, you can see that the bend is pretty straight along the center of the photo.

STEP 2:

Select the Magnetic Lasso tool from the Toolbox (or just press L until you have it). It's located under the Lasso tool group. Make sure the Edge Contrast is set to 10% in the Options Bar.

STEP 3:

Press Z to get the Zoom tool and click on the bend to zoom in on it, then press L to return to the Magnetic Lasso tool. Click the mouse button once on the bottom edge of the start of the bend on the left side of the photo, then drag slowly along the bend from left to right. You should see a little line appear that snaps to the edges of the bend as you drag. If any part of the line snaps to an area other then the bend, just press the Backspace (Mac: Delete) key to remove it and go back. To add a point in a specific place, just click the mouse button in that spot, then go back to dragging along the bend.

STEP 4:

When you get to the right edge, press-and-hold the Alt (Mac: Option) key to switch to the regular Lasso tool. Then click-and-drag downward to the bottom, then over to the left, and then up to the point where you started in Step 3 to close the selection off. Make sure you hold the Alt key down as you're dragging.

Continued

STEP 5:

Now that you have a selection over the bottom half of the photo, press Ctrl-J (Mac: Command-J) to copy that part of the photo onto its own layer.

STEP 6:

Make sure the top layer is active in the Layers palette. Press Ctrl-T (Mac: Command-T) to go into Free Transform mode. Click on the top-middle box and drag it upward until you don't see the bend anymore. Don't click the check-mark yet, though. We're not done.

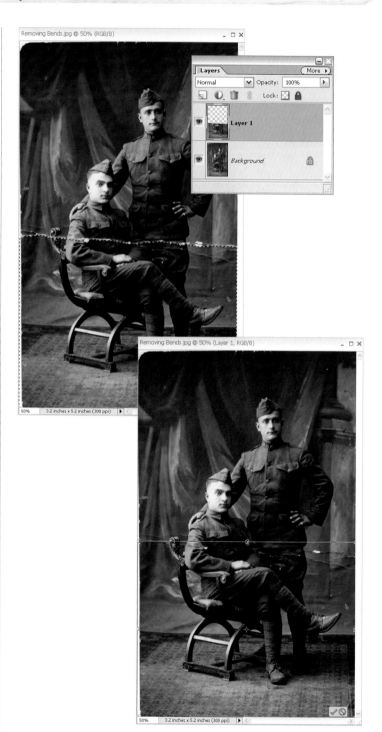

STEP 7:

You'll probably notice that parts of the photo on the left (the arm) and right (the leg) look like they don't match up.

STEP 8:

Ctrl-click (Mac: Command-click) on the top-left corner point of the bounding box and drag it inward slightly until the arm matches up with the rest of itself. Do the same on the right side if needed.

Continued

STEP 9:
Click on the green checkmark at the bottom of the bounding box to commit the transformation. Press the little Eye icon on the top layer to turn it on and off to see the difference. You could always go in and use the Clone Stamp tool (S), like we have in the last two tutorials, to fix some of the bend areas that weren't fixed here.

TIP: This technique probably seems a little too easy. Well it is. But, keep something in mind here. Think of who your audience is. The people who see this work won't be looking at the small details. They'll be absolutely thrilled to see their memories preserved. You may know what the original photo looked like but no one else does. They won't be able to see the small seam that may have been created because we cheated here. It's either that or spend a whole lot of time cloning and healing. Me personally, I'd rather move on to a photo that needed some more work and rest easy knowing that I cheated a little and saved myself a lot of time.

Before

After

Continued

METHOD 2: A More Controlled Technique

If your bends and cracks don't fall along a straight line or there are numerous ones in the photo, then you'll probably need to use a more controlled technique.

STEP 1:

Here, I'm starting out with a photo that has bends, creases, and cracks in several places.

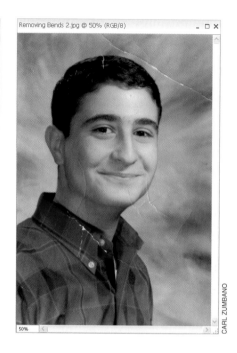

STEP 2:

First, click on the Create a New Layer icon at the top of the Layers palette to create a new blank layer.

STEP 3:

Select the Healing Brush tool from the Toolbox, or press J until you have it. It's right under the Spot Healing Brush. Make sure that the Sample All Layers checkbox is turned on in the top Options Bar.

STEP 4:

Remember that the Healing Brush tool requires a sample area to work from. Click once on the blank top layer that you just created to make sure it is selected. Now, press-and-hold the Alt (Mac: Option) key and click in a non-bent area of the background to select a sample to work with. Make sure you click somewhere close to the bent area so the lighting and texture are similar.

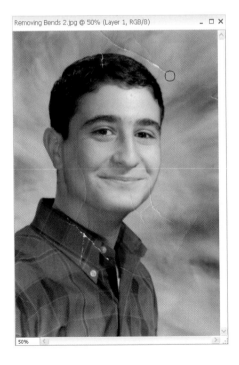

STEP 5:

Click and start painting next to the area you just sampled. Notice how the Healing brush melds the two areas together.

Continued

STEP 6:

Now move on to another part of the photo. Let's save the face for last, though. Here, I'm moving to another part of the background. Remember that the Healing Brush works by using a sampled area, so you'll need to resample when you move to another area. Press-and-hold the Alt (Mac: Option) key again and click to sample near the area you're going to fix. Then click-and-paint over the bend to meld it in with the clean background around it. You can fix the rest of the background the same way and you'll even be able to fix the hair with the same tool as well.

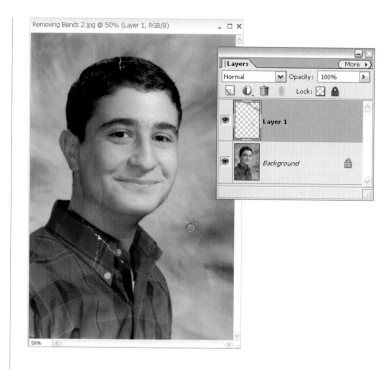

STEP 7:

Let's now move on to the face and skin area. For the most part, the Healing Brush will work fine here as well. Especially, in the large open areas. Zoom in if you need to, then use the Healing Brush to sample a clean area of skin and paint over the bend next to it. Elements will meld the two together pretty seamlessly.

STEP 8:

Unfortunately, some of the bends extend from the skin over to the background. That's where it gets tricky. The strategy is slightly different for this part. While the Healing Brush works great for the background and areas of the skin, I find it doesn't work as well when the texture changes from the skin to the background. Here's an example of what happened when I tried the Healing Brush on the chin where the bend extended into the background. Not so great, huh?

STEP 9:

So, let's press S to switch to the Clone Stamp tool. Again, make sure that the Sample All Layers checkbox is turned on in the Options Bar. From the Brush Picker, select a small, soft-edged brush that is about twice the size of the bend you're painting over. Just like the Healing Brush tool, we need to sample from a clean area, so press-and-hold the Alt (Mac: Option) key and click to sample a clean area of skin along the edge of the face just above the bend.

Continued

STEP 10:

Now click to clone over the bend. If you don't get the edge of the skin just right, press Ctrl-Z (Mac: Command-Z) to Undo and try again. It may take a couple tries, but it's worth it to get a nice clean edge.

STEP 11:

Finally, work on the shirt to finish things up. Again, I've used the Clone Stamp tool here, since I don't want to meld areas together. Instead, I want to create an exact copy of the pattern on the shirt so the Clone Stamp tool is the guy for the job.

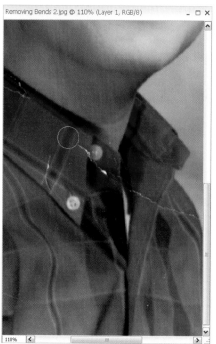

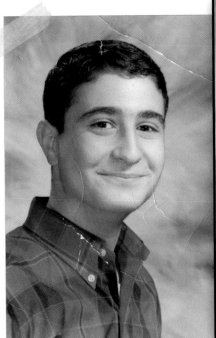

Before

After

Adding in Missing People

Everyone has a photo that they wish could have another loved one in it with them. Well, we can't turn back time and retake the photo, but we can do the next best thing and use Elements to put people together in the same photo.

STEP 1:

Open the two photos containing the people you'd like to unite. Here's a photo of my grandmother in her front yard and another one of my mother in the same yard. Unfortunately, they either didn't have a photo taken together or that photo is lost. Regardless, neither of them has a nice photo of the two of them when my mom was young, and they both really wanted one. As the resident Photoshop Elements expert, I was called in for the task.

TIP: When your friends and family get wind that you have some Elements skills, you'll undoubtedly be called in for similar work. In fact, your family may well work you until the wee hours of the morning in the name of love. I have two suggestions for you: (1) VAULT™ energy drink. I've recently discovered it while writing this book. Other than the occasional twitching I get now and then, I find it helps keep me working like a champ. (2) Lie your butt off to get out of the work. Deny any association with Elements and the computer for that matter. In fact, throw this book away every time they come over. It's cheap enough, you can just go by the bookstore to pick up another copy when they leave.

STEP 2:

First, decide which photo will become the main photo and which one will become the photo you steal a person from. Here, I've decided to move my mother into the photo of my grandmother. Click once on the photo that has the person you'd like to move. This brings that photo to the front. Make sure you can still see the other photo offset behind this one, though.

STEP 3:

Press L to select the Lasso tool and draw a quick, rough selection around the person you are going to move to the other photo.

Continued

STEP 4:

Now press V to select the Move tool and position your cursor inside the selection. You'll see a bounding box surrounding your selection.

STEP 5:

Click-and-drag that selection over on top of the other photo and release your mouse button. You'll see just the selected portion of the photo move with your cursor as you drag. Don't release your mouse button until you get over the other photo, though.

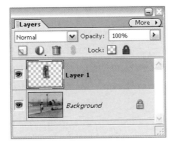

STEP 6:

As soon as you release your mouse button, you'll see a new layer was added to the Layers palette of the main photo.

STEP 7:

Click once on the new layer that you just brought into the main photo to make sure it is selected. Now press E to select the Eraser tool. Choose a medium-sized, hard-edged brush and start erasing away the areas around the copied photo that don't belong. Don't go too close to the edges at this point. Just get the large stuff and leave the edges for the next step.

STEP 8:

Now select a small, soft-edged brush. Again, with the Eraser tool get closer to the edges and erase away any remnants from the original background of the copied photo. The goal here is to isolate the woman so the layer only has her body on it. If you have trouble seeing the outline of the woman's body, you can always press V to switch back to the Move tool and move her to a more contrasting part of the background, or click on the Eye icon next to the Background layer in the Layers palette to hide the rest of the image.

Continued

STEP 9:

Great, the hard part is done. If the people don't match in size, press Ctrl-T (Mac: Command-T) to go into Free Transform mode.

STEP 10:

Press-and-hold the Shift key to keep your resizing proportional, then click-and-drag one of the corner handles inward to shrink the size of the added person and match the size of the original person. Click on the small green check-mark to commit the transformation.

STEP 11:

Now all you need to do is decide if you want to put the new person in front of the person in the main photo or behind them. I tried putting my mom in front and I think it looked too fake. Take a look and see for yourself.

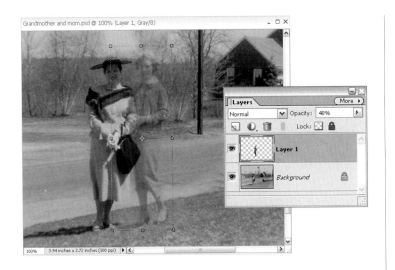

STEP 12:

Since I'm not crazy about the way it looks when she's in front of my grandmother, let's put her behind. Position the photo where you'd like it. Then change the Opacity setting of the top layer to 40% in the Layers palette. This will help you see the person in the main photo but also see the person you're adding in as well.

STEP 13:

Select the Eraser tool and choose a small, hard-edged brush in the Brush Picker. Start painting over the places where the photo you're adding intersects with the person in the main photo. Take your time here. If you mess up and inadvertently erase something you didn't want to, just press Ctrl-Z (Mac: Command-Z) to Undo and try again.

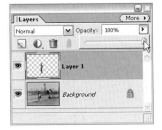

STEP 14:

Once you're done erasing, change the Opacity setting of the top layer back to 100%.

Continued

STEP 15:

Okay, we're looking pretty good here. You could stop here, but we don't just want this to look good—we want it to be convincing. One thing that makes this change look a bit fake is the lack of a shadow between the two women. If they were really that close together, there would be some type of shadow cast from the woman in front onto the woman in the back.

STEP 16:

To add the shadow, first Ctrl-click (Mac: Command-click) on the layer thumbnail of the person we just added. This will put a selection around that person.

STEP 17:

Now click on the Create a New Layer icon at the top of the Layers palette to create a new blank layer. Don't deselect yet.

STEP 18:

Press B to select the Brush tool. Choose a small, soft-edged brush that is about the size of the shadow you want to cast. Then press the letter D to set your Foreground color to black. Now paint a quick, black brush stroke on the inside of the selection edge.

STEP 19:

Press Ctrl-D (Mac: Command-D) to Deselect. Reduce the Opacity setting of the shadow layer to about 45%. Now the image looks much more believable. See, now aren't you happy you took those extra steps to take this image to the next level?

Continued

Before

After

A wise man once said, "A good man knows his limits." Okay, I actually got that from a Clint Eastwood movie, but hey, it works here, too. The idea behind that quote is that you, too, should know your limits. There's no glamour in spending six hours restoring a photo just for the heck of it. Especially if the focal point of that photo is a person in the middle and the bulk of the work you do is on the background. In those cases, I have one simple tool to help out: the Crop tool.

Cropping Difficult-to-Fix Areas

WORKMAN FAMILY ARCHIVE

STEP 1:
Well folks, this one is short and sweet. Open a photo that's got the subject set on a fairly significant and large background that has a lot of damage to it—damage that you might normally think you should try to restore and repair.

STEP 2:
Press C to select the Crop tool from the Toolbox. Then just click-and-drag around the focus of your photo to crop the bad areas out. You'll see a semi-opaque gray area around the crop you just created. That is the area that will be removed. The clear area in the middle is what will be saved.

Continued

STEP 3:

If you need to make changes to the cropping area you just made, then click-and-drag any of the corner handles to resize the crop box or click-and-drag inside the box to move it. If you're done, just press the little green check-mark at the bottom of the crop box to crop the photo.

TIP: I know you're thinking to your-self, "That's it?" Yep. That's all there is to it. Why spend a lot of time repair-ing the background when it's really an insignificant part of the photo? After all, your friends or family are really only concerned about one thing here—the people in the photo. That's where the memories come from and that's what they want to preserve. So, make it easier on yourself and forget about the parts of the photo that don't matter as much.

Before

After

Here's another one of those circumstances where the fix is really simple and straightforward. Many times, the edges of the photo and the background fade or show extreme signs of aging. Instead of trying to repair them, try this technique of adding a vignette to hide the damage and bring attention to the subject in the center of the photo.

Enhancing Damaged or Faded Edges

STEP 1:

Here, I've opened a beautiful photo that was kept in great condition. However, the edges of the photo have this faded, noisy look to them. Especially near the bottom of the photo.

STEP 2:

Instead of trying to clone and heal the photo, why not just minimize the effect the edges of the photo have on the overall picture? Go under the Filter menu and choose Correct Camera Distortion.

Continued

TIP: Have you ever looked under the Filter menu and seen the item you want grayed out? If so, your photo may have been scanned or captured as a grayscale photo and not an RGB color photo. You can check this (and change it for that matter) by going under the Image menu to Mode. Make sure that RGB Color is the checked image mode on the menu.

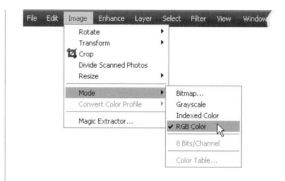

STEP 3:

When the Correct Camera Distortion dialog opens, the first thing I usually do is uncheck the Show Grid checkbox at the bottom right of the preview area. I personally find it very loud and distracting. However, if you like loud and distracting things, then by all means keep it turned on. Now, loud and distracting aside, under the Vignette section, go ahead and drag the Amount slider over to the left to darken those damaged edges.

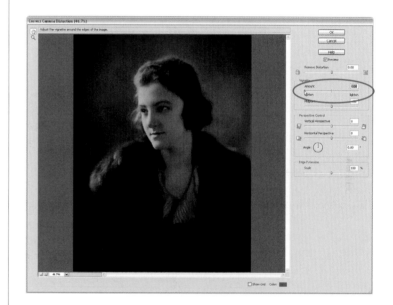

STEP 4:

Finally, drag the Midpoint slider to the left as well, to make the darkened edges encroach even more toward the center of the photo. This setting really depends on how much area your subject has in the photo. Don't move it too far, or you'll start to darken them as well. Click OK and now you've got an easy fix for those faded edges.

Before

After

Don't Fix the Background— Move the Person

Weird name for a tutorial, huh? Honestly, I just couldn't think of a better one. I mean, the name does say it all here. If you've got a messy background, why try to fix it? Select the person from the background and just move them onto a new one. We'll create our own background here but it could just as easily be a background that already exists. Here's a modification of a trick I saw Katrin Eismann do at a Photoshop World Conference.

STEP 1:

Open a photo that has a background that needs fixing. Here, the background almost looks like some black mist that you'd see out of a horror movie. Not sure what happened, but it's fairly distracting. Instead of fixing it, let's just go ahead and create a new background and move the subject onto it.

STEP 2:

Let's start out by creating the background first. In the existing portrait, go to the Select menu and choose Select All (or just press Ctrl-A [Mac: Command-A]) to select everything. Choose Edit>Copy to copy the photo to the clipboard. Then press Ctrl-D (Mac: Command-D) to Deselect.

STEP 3:

Now choose File>New>Blank File to create a new document. Elements will create a new document that is exactly the size of the image you just copied. Just click OK to create the blank image.

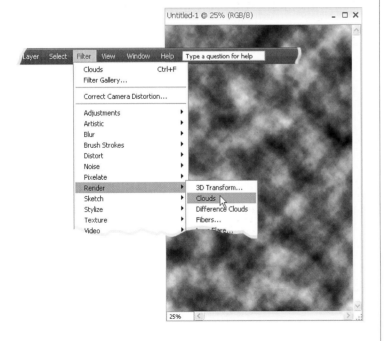

STEP 4:

Press the letter D to set your Foreground and Background to their default colors—black and white. Then choose Filter>Render>Clouds. This creates a cloudy texture on the background document.

Continued

STEP 5:

Choose Filter>Blur>Motion Blur. Use an Angle setting of 70° and set the Distance to a large number, such as 800 pixels. Click OK to apply the filter.

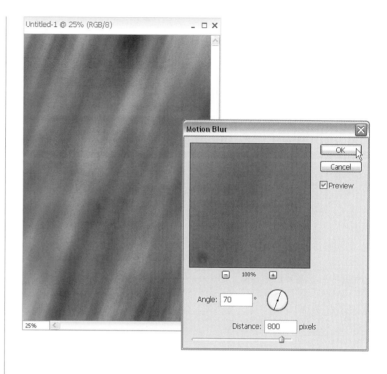

STEP 6:

Now go to the Filter menu again, and choose Blur>Gaussian Blur. Set the Radius to 30 pixels and click OK to blur the background even more.

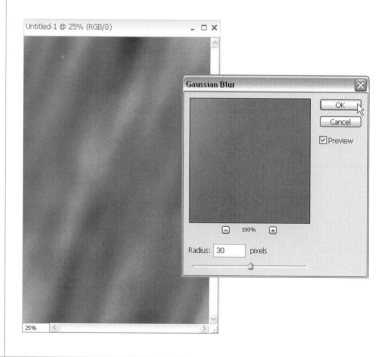

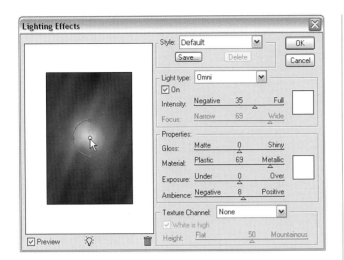

STEP 7:

Okay, the new background is almost done. Go to the Filter menu one last time and choose Render>Lighting Effects. First, choose Omni from the pop-up menu for the Light Type setting. Then click on the small, white circle in the middle of the light in the preview area on the left. Drag this circle so it appears around the place where your subject will appear (usually in the center).

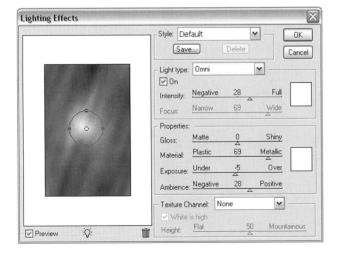

STEP 8:

Adjust the other settings depending on how light or dark you want the spotlight. You can get creative here or just use the settings that I've used. For the first time go ahead and use my settings, but I do encourage you to experiment with your own settings, as you can come up with some pretty cool lighting effects.

Continued

STEP 9:

Click OK when you're done to apply the filter and now you've got a custom background ready for your subject.

STEP 10:

Now click on the actual photo of the person that you're going to move to switch image windows. Go under the Image menu and choose Magic Extractor.

STEP 11:

This dialog is a great way to select objects or people from the background. First, use the Foreground Brush tool (the marker with the plus sign next to it) to paint on the person. This tells Elements that you want to keep this part of the photo.

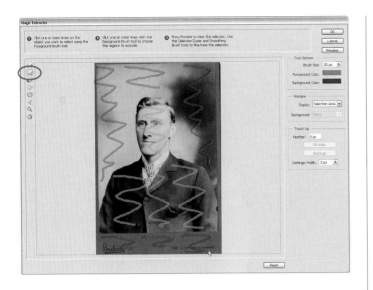

STEP 12:

Then, click on the Background Brush tool (the marker with the minus sign next to it) and paint over the background. This tells Elements that you want to remove this area.

STEP 13:

Now, click on the Preview button at the top right to see Elements extract the person from the background.

STEP 14:

Most of the time Elements does a good job of removing the person. Once in a while though, it may remove part of the person as it did here with the very top of the hair and along the right side.

Continued

STEP 15:

If this happens to you, select the Add to Selection tool (the little paintbrush on top of a circle) on the left side of the dialog. Then, click-and-paint in the areas you want to add back to your photo (like the hair here).

STEP 16:

If you've inadvertently clicked on an area you didn't really want to add or Elements didn't extract all of the background, then you can manually erase it by selecting the Remove From Selection tool and painting on those areas (like the background above the shoulder).

STEP 17:

The last thing I do before exiting the dialog is click the Defringe button on the middle right. Fringes, or the outline that may appear around the photo, are a dead giveaway to faked work, so it's good to get rid of them. In fact, you may not even see the fringing but I usually click the button once anyway, just to be sure.

STEP 18:

Click OK when you're done and you should have your subject separated away from the background.

Move To Simple Background.jpg @ 25% (Laye...

25%

Continued

STEP 19:

Press V to select the Move tool. Then click on the subject and drag it over onto the other image document that you created for the background.

TIP: If you press-and-hold the Shift key while you move your extracted image, Elements will automatically place it in the center of the new document when you drop it onto that document.

STEP 20:

If you find the subject is too small for the image since you removed some of the background, just press Ctrl-T (Mac: Command-T) to bring up Free Transform and click on a corner handle to make it slightly larger. Press-and-hold the Shift key while you drag the corner point to keep your image proportional. Click the little green checkmark to commit the transformation when you're done (or just press the Enter [Mac: Return] key). Add a little edge darkening (see the previous tutorial) and you've got a great portrait.

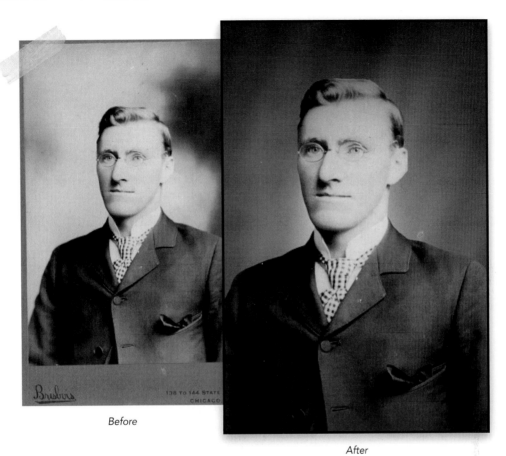

Before

After

Appendix

Getting Your Photos Onto Your Computer

In this chapter. I'm going to show you how to get your photos onto your computer. A word of advice: if you've already got them there, then just skip this chapter. It's pretty short and it's just here to show you the basics. However, if you don't know how to get all of the photos you'd like to work with on your computer, then you will probably want to read through it. Especially if you'll be scanning photos, or have a lot of older photos that you'd like to restore.

Getting Photos from a Camera or Card Reader

Here's the easiest of all ways to get photos from your camera onto your computer. In fact, I'd say that it doesn't get much easier than this. If you've got a digital camera and you've taken some photos, then the tutorial you're about to read will show you how to transfer them onto your computer. Now, if the photos you have aren't on a digital camera and you need to scan them, then feel free to skip this one and go to the next tutorial to find out how.

METHOD 1: Using a Card Reader

This is actually the way most people prefer to get photos onto the computer. First of all, it's really easy because you can purchase a card reader at just about any type of electronics store. Next, it's somewhat safer than connecting your camera directly to the computer because you can risk losing photos if, say, your camera battery runs out during the transfer.

©ISTOCKPHOTO/STEVEN TULISSI

STEP 1:

First, remove your memory card from your camera and place it into the card reader.

STEP 2:

Your computer will probably think for a moment or two, and then you'll see the Adobe Photo Downloader pop up (assuming you already have Photoshop Elements installed on your computer).

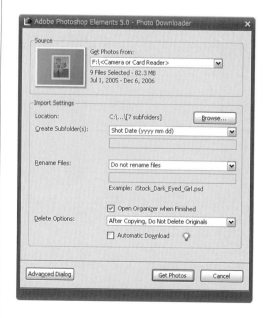

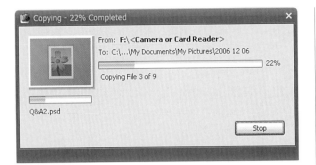

STEP 3:

Select the photos that you want to download and click on the Get Photos button. The download process will begin and you'll see a smaller dialog with a progress bar appear. This can take anywhere from a few seconds to a few minutes—it'll just depend on how many photos you have on your memory card. *Note:* Some cards can hold up to 8 GB, and if the card is full, you may want to go have a cup of coffee (or four) while the photos are transferring.

METHOD 2: Connecting the Camera Directly to the Computer

Most cameras come with a cable that connects the camera directly to the computer. This method is okay, but it has two disadvantages: (1) it's usually slower than using a card reader, and (2) it's prone to errors, since if something happens when the photos are transferring (like the battery in the camera goes dead), you may lose your photos.

©ISTOCKPHOTO/TOM GUFLER

STEP 1:

Connect the cable from the camera to the computer.

Continued

STEP 2:

Your computer will probably think for a moment or two, and then you'll see the Adobe Photo Downloader pop up.

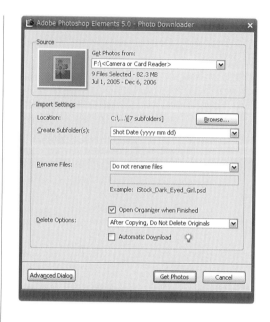

STEP 3:

Select the photos that you want to download and click on the Get Photos button. The download process will begin and you'll see a smaller dialog with a progress bar appear. As I mentioned earlier, it's slower than the previous method, so expect to wait as much as double the amount of time as you would when using a card reader.

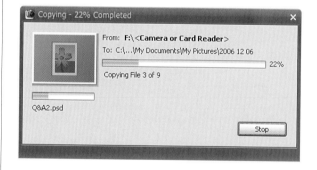

So, you've been shooting digital photos for a while now. You have all of your recent memories on the computer but you're missing something. You keep thinking how you'd love to do something more with some of those older photos. That's where a flatbed scanner comes in. A flatbed scanner scans photos onto your computer in a manner similar to a photocopier. Now, it doesn't matter how old these photos are—one year old or 100 years old. If they're not digital, then you'll need another way to get them on your computer and a scanner is it.

Scanning New or Old Photos Into Your Computer

MATT KLOSKOWSKI

STEP 1:
I hate to mention the obvious here, but you'll need a flatbed scanner to start. You can get a great scanner for under a hundred bucks from any electronics or computer store. However, as with many things in life, you get what you pay for. I actually use the Epson Perfection V750-M PRO. It costs a little more than some of the cheaper ones you'll find out there, but let me tell ya—it's worth every penny. The scanning speed and quality of image that this scanner produces blows the other ones out of the water.

MATT KLOSKOWSKI

STEP 2:
Get the photo (or photos) that you want to scan and place it on the scanner. If you're scanning multiple photos (also called a "gang" scan), place as many as you can fit, but be sure to keep them at least ¼-inch apart so they don't overlap.

Continued

STEP 3:

Inside Elements, choose File>Import>Your Scanner's Name. This will most likely launch a scan dialog where you can tweak the settings for scanning. Here's where it gets a little tricky, but I'll show you what to look out for. First and foremost, the main thing we'll need to be concerned about is the resolution setting. If you're thinking about printing this photo, then you'll want to set the resolution to 300 dpi. That's actually a bit higher than you'll need, but not by much and it gives you some wiggle room later in Elements, in case you need it.

TIP: Most scanning software will do some automatic corrections for you. I encourage you to stay away from those settings. Photoshop Elements is a much better tool for getting the best results. After all, Elements was built for that; your scanning software was not. Plus, you have this book and I show you how to fix the same things that the scanning software will try to, but better.

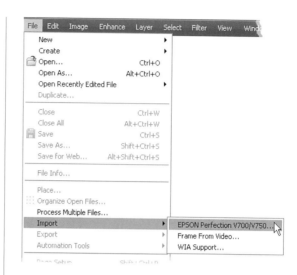

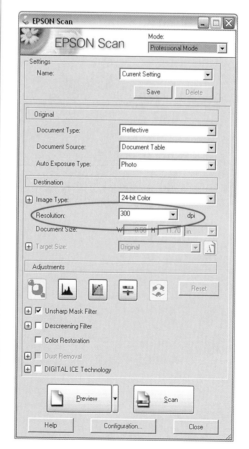

CARL ZUMBANO, CARLINE ZUMBANO, AND MARK RIELAND

STEP 4:
Most scanning software has a Preview button somewhere near the actual Scan button. Go ahead and click it to preview your scan just to make sure that it looks as expected.

Continued

STEP 5:

When you're satisfied that the photo(s) is placed correctly and is ready to be scanned, press the Scan button. The time this takes really depends on the quality of your scanner. The Epson Perfection V750-M PRO takes about 20 seconds, but I've owned scanners that can take as long as a few minutes. When it's done, you'll have a new image window open in the Elements Editor. First things first: save the image by choosing File>Save As. Give it a descriptive name, choose the PSD format, and click Save. Now it's on your computer and you're ready to roll (when I say "roll," I mean you're ready to move on to the rest of the book).

TIP: At this point, you may be wondering how the heck you're going to extract each photo from the scan if you've scanned multiple photos together. Well, make sure you read on to the next tutorial to find out, because I've got one killer trick to show you.

Okay, at the end of the previous tutorial, I mentioned I had a killer trick to help you when you're scanning multiple photos. I've got to tell you that this trick totally rocks! You'll be amazed at the time it saves. In fact, I've seen two emotions come to light when I show this: (1) extreme happiness, and (2) extreme anger. The anger is mostly from the folks who never knew this trick existed and spent countless hours manually dividing scanned photos.

Dividing and Cropping Multi-Photo Scans

STEP 1:

Let's say you've scanned several photos like the document shown here. While I was scanning, I was careful to include at least ⅛-inch of space (preferably ¼-inch) between each photo. Once the image is in Elements, go to the Image menu and choose Divide Scanned Photos.

Continued

STEP 2:

You'll see Elements do some fancy work on the screen for a minute and then, almost magically, you'll see that all of your photos are in separate documents. How's that for service? Now you don't have to worry about it. Just save all those photos as PSD files (File>Save As) and you're ready to roll (you should already know what I mean by that).

The first time I taught this technique, I forgot to mention the most important part—why? Needless to say, I was met with many puzzled looks. So, why in the world would you take a photo of a photo? Well, without getting too technical, a scanner uses light when it scans your photo. Some photos, especially old ones, have a reflective coating on them that doesn't turn out too well on a scanner. So, you'll need another way. Taking a photo of a photo is it.

Taking Photos of Old Photos

SNYDER FAMILY ARCHIVE

©ISTOCKPHOTO/ANDY PIATT

STEP 1:
This is actually more technique than it is Photoshop Elements, but I think it's important given the subject of this book. I've started by scanning the photo first to give you an idea of what it looks like when scanned. As you can see, that reflective surface has wreaked havoc on the photo.

TIP: Try to straighten the photo as much as possible. Photographing a bent photo will automatically put you at a disadvantage, so do your best to straighten it out. Maybe even try sticking it in the pages of a thick book overnight.

STEP 2:
One of the most important aspects here is keeping the camera absolutely still. To do this you'll need a tripod, regardless of whether you're shooting with a point-and-shoot digital camera or a digital SLR. If you don't have a tripod, then consider putting the camera on a bookshelf, table, or any other flat surface that'll keep it totally still.

Continued

STEP 3:

Next, you'll need to set the photo up. There are two essential keys for getting a good photo of a photo. First, make sure the photo is straight in front of your camera when you're shooting it—at a 90° angle to either the floor (if you're using a tripod) or the flat surface your camera is resting on. You can lay the photo flat and shoot straight down at it, if you can set your camera up with a stable way to do that or you have a special piece of equipment that points your camera straight down, since a tripod won't allow you to shoot straight down on the photo. Either way, you need to make sure your lens is pointed straight at the photo and the camera is stable. So, I suggest using the tripod or whatever flat surface you have and taping or pinning the photo up on a wall, so you can still shoot straight at the photo—it's not straight down but it's still totally fine.

MATT KLOSKOWSKI

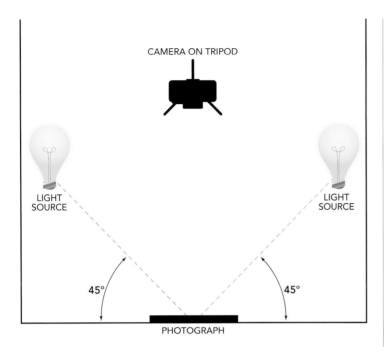

CAMERA ON TRIPOD

LIGHT SOURCE

LIGHT SOURCE

45°   45°

PHOTOGRAPH

STEP 4:

Now let's talk about lighting. You may think you need a pro lighting setup, but you don't. First and foremost though, turn the flash on the camera off. It'll bounce light right back at the lens and give you worse reflections and lighting than you'd get if you scanned the photo. Even light is the best here and you can get that with some subtle indirect sunlight, like the kind you get from a covered window (just don't place the photo too close to the window). You could also use the light you'd get from a lamp, as long as the lamp isn't too close to the photo. Either way, try to place the light at a 45° angle to the photo. Even better, if you have two light sources, place them on either side of the photo at 45° angles.

TIP: Hallways make for great lighting. It's almost like a fake lightbox, if you've got some windows nearby and you can get enough light inside it.

STEP 5:

You're ready to take the shot, so go ahead and try it. It may take a few attempts at adjusting the lighting and exposure settings on the camera, until you get it right. When you do get it right, I suggest writing a quick note of what setup you used so you don't forget if you have to do it again one day. When you're done, just follow the tutorials earlier in this chapter for getting the photos from your camera onto your computer.

Index

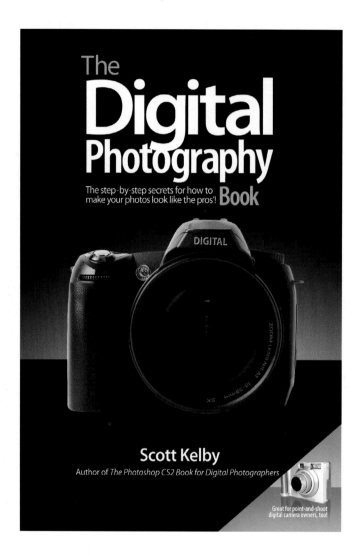

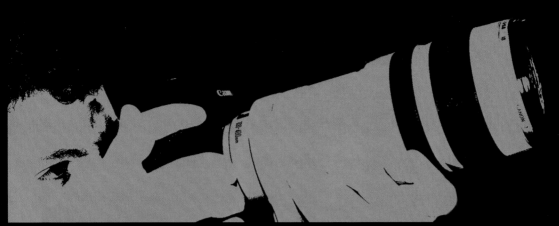

BEFORE

SMOOTH SAILING
Adobe Photoshop Elements Techniques makes it easy!

Chart a new course for your photos with *Adobe Photoshop Elements Techniques* newsletter and website. Learn how to:

- Enhance color and lighting
- Create mind-blowing effects
- Edit and retouch images
- Restore or repair heirloom photographs
- Organize and print your photos

Plus, get access to an exclusive subscriber-only website with a boatload of helpful tutorials; download free styles, brushes and shapes; or create and share your own image gallery. *Check it out!*

Limited Time Offer, Subscribe Today!

One-Year Subscription
$**49**[*] Plus get **50%** off the Portrait Retouching with Photoshop Elements DVD (pay just $19.99)
Use promotional code: ELEN-1UPCP

Two-Year Subscription
$**79**[*] And get the Portrait Retouching with Photoshop Elements DVD ($39.99 value) **FREE!**
Use promotional code: ELEN-2UPCP

To subscribe call **866-808-2793** or visit **www.photoshopelementsuser.com**

*Prices in U.S. funds. International and Canadian pricing is available online. Adobe and Photoshop are registered trademarks of Adobe Systems Incorporated.